D1339924

Collecting
Susie Cooper

Francis Joseph

First impression

Published in the UK by
Francis Joseph Publications
15 St Swithuns Road, London SE13 6RW

Typeset, printed and bound in Great Britain by
E J Folkard Print Services
199 Station Road, Crayford, Kent DA1 3QF

ISBN 1-870703-96-0

Acknowledgements

This book has been put together by the efforts of a small number of dedicated people, without whom the information, colour plates and listings in this book would not have been possible. They are warmly thanked for their contributions.

They are:

Nick Jones and
Geoffrey Peake

Alfies Antiques Market
Unit G070-4, 13-25 Church Street,
Marylebone, London NW8
Tel: 0171 723 0449

Beverley & Beth

Beverley
30 Church Street, Marylebone,
London NW8
0171-262 1576

Trevor Leek

Photography, London, 0181-293 4440

Pat and Howard Watson

Stalls 3 & 4, Stratford Antique Centre,
Ely Stree, Stratford-on-Avon CV37 6LN
Tel: 01789 204351 or 01789 299524 (Home)

Mark Wilkinson and
Jane Hay

Christies South Kensington
85 Old Brompton Road, London SW7 3LD
Tel: 0171-581 7611

Lindsay Bartrop-White
K J White

Tel: 01920 484013

Production
Francis Salmon
Clare Ling
John Folkard

Foreword

In the pages of this book, those uninitiated, as well as those who are ardent admirers of Susie Cooper will find useful information and extensive colour reproductions of her work. With its informal style, this book is approachable for collectors and traders alike.

This is truly a 'collectors' guide, having a format which makes it accessable and easy to understand — thus providing everything for the admirer of Susie Cooper designs.

There is a price guide towards the end of the book which is designed to give readers a general indication as to the current market value of Susie Cooper's work. This is intentionally brief, as the market for Susie Cooper's work changes all the time, and a very detailed guide would soon be out of date. Experts in the field are a good source of valuations, some of whom are mentioned in this book. Please remember, also, that dealers will have to have some form of mark-up on the value of any piece, so if you are a collector there is likely to be a difference between the buying price, and the resale price of any purchase you make. However, with Susie Cooper's work being so collectable today, and with there being only a limited supply, it would be reasonable to assume that any purchase you make has 'investment' potential.

Contents

Studio Vase circa 1933

Studio Vase, circa 1932/33

1930's Ibex Plate, silver Unicorn beaker, Fox or Hound.

SVC banded 'Cosy' shape teapot, mid 1930s.

INTRODUCTION

One of the unique characteristics of Susie Cooper pottery is the breadth of time over which it has been produced. No other designer has covered the seven decades of design we have seen from Susie Cooper. She reflects with total sensitivity the design ideas of the periods through which she worked, allied with a down-to-earth appreciation of the needs of the housewife. As the 1930s advertising slogan put it, *'Elegance combined with utility. Artistry associated with commerce and practicality'*.

A wide variety of work is still readily available, ranging from her early earthenware to the fine bone china of post-war years, with all kinds of decoration — freehand painting, aerographing, tube-lining, lithographs, crayon patterns, lustre decoration, sgraffito and incised ware.

It has been estimated that she produced over 4500 patterns and about 500 new shapes, so there is likely to be something that will appeal to every collector of ceramics among her work.

The price range is equally wide ranging from a few pounds to over a thousand for rare examples at auction. Space requirements can be tailored to availability — plates can be attractively displayed on a wall, coffee cans can be grouped on a small set of shelves, a dinner service can fill a dresser, a single vase can highlight a colour scheme.

Her work fits equally well into modern or traditional interiors. Because of its subtle colours and classic shapes it has an understated elegance that is tasteful and timeless. Her work is still emerging in sufficient quantity to find perfect examples in almost all areas, so it is possible to set high standards for a collection and to reject worn or damaged pieces. However, if an item is very rare, one may have to accept it in the condition it comes.

Since her work spans the Art Deco period, now very collectable, and the newly collectable Forties and Fifties as well as more recent decades, examples can be found at all levels — at general antiques fairs, antique centres and markets and at specialist Art Deco shops and fairs across the country. With a vast amount exported to America, this is also true in the United States.

Susie Coop er has become so popular that there is even a collectors group with a newsletter offering the opportunity to advertise items for sale or items wanted and giving information about exhibitions and specialist auctions of her work. Her work is instantly recognisable and can be picked out easily when it turns up in unpromising circumstances like flea-markets and charity shops. Though this now happens less often, it is part of the joy of collecting to suddenly come across a 'find'.

Backstamps and pattern numbers help dating, while the style of decoration also helps to indicate the period of production. Occasionally a pattern name may be added, but more often than not there is no set pattern name, and many of her hand-painted designs are referred to only as "Geometric". Her latest designs have been for tapestry and felt applique, which can be used to complement her ceramic work. Very rare examples of her work can be seen in national collections like the Victoria and Albert Museum in London or The City Museum and Art Gallery, Hanley, Stoke-on-Trent.

Suitable items can be chosen for display in every room of the house, including the bathroom. If a change of direction in collecting is indicated, unwanted items can be easily disposed of, often at a profit.

Incomplete sets can often be made up with the help of a china matching service, and, at present, prices are such that it is possible to make use of dinner, tea and coffee services — if not in everyday use, at least for special occasions. Given the quantity of items still available, the question of fakes seems unlikely to arise. The only proviso for the collector is to ensure that on early handpainted geometric patterns the painting is original, since these were subject to flaking and may have been repainted, though this is fairly easily detected with experience.

Because of the length of her career and her versatility in owning and designing for her own factory (very unusual in the Thirties), many articles have been written about Susie Cooper and these can form an interesting ancillary collection. Similarly background information covering the whole of her career can be obtained from studying the works listed in the bibliography of this book. Our aim is to give the collector a practical introduction to the work of Britain's leading lady of the Potteries, and it is hoped that this will stimulate yet further interest in her considerable achievements.

A BRIEF BIOGRAPHY

Susan Vera Cooper was born at Stansfield, near Burslem, on 29th October, 1902. She was the youngest of seven children and had three brothers and three sisters. Her great-grandparents had had connections with the pottery industry, but her parents ran a farm and a family retail business.

An early interest in drawing and painting led her to evening classes at the Burslem School of Art where she studied freehand painting and plant form. She was encouraged by her mother and her tutor, ceramic artist and designer Gordon Forsyth, and she went on to win a scholarship for full-time tuition.

Initially interested in textile and fashion design, she decided to apply for a scholarship to the Royal College of Art in London in 1922, but to qualify for this she needed industrial experience.

Gordon Forsyth advised her to take employment at the pottery decorating firm of A. E. Gray, beginning as a paintress on piece-work. This gave her invaluable experience of work on the factory floor. She was soon promoted to designing on an hourly rate and then became resident designer, becoming as she later said, "committed to local industry".

She stayed at Grays for around seven years, designing brightly-coloured geometric, floral and banded ware, which was marked with a backstamp of an ocean liner incorporating the words, *Designed by Susie Cooper*. She also during this time produced textile designs for Skelhorn and Edwards, a London-based firm.

Ambitious and confident of her capabilities, she found it irksome to be inhibited by what the firm's sales force believed would sell, and by the limited range of shapes available to her.

In order to have greater freedom to ensure harmony between shape and pattern she decided the only way forward was as an independent pottery producer and she left Gray's on her twenty-seventh birthday.

With the backing of her family and with her brother-in-law Jack Beeson (known as 'Uncle Jack') who became her business partner, she set up at the *George Street Pottery*, Tunstall. This was the autumn of

1929 which was also the year of the Wall Street Crash, and unfortunately her landlord became bankrupt. This left her without premises, but undeterred, in the spring of 1930 she moved to the Chelsea Works in Moorland Road, Burslem, renting space from Royal Doulton. She bought in whiteware for which she designed simple patterns that were within the capabilities of her young workforce. These included **Polka Dot**, **Exclamation Mark** and banded patterns.

At the British Industries Fair of 1931, her work created considerable interest and, impressed by this, Harry Wood of Wood and Sons offered her not only more convenient premises at his Crown Works in Burslem but also facilities for the production of shapes to her own design. She took up the offer and her first shapes were reminiscent of birds including *Kestrel* and *Curlew* (1932) and *Falcon* and *Spiral* (1937). They were not only highly stylised and innovative, but they were also easy to clean, with spouts that poured well. This was also true of *Wren*, *Jay* and *Rex* (1935) which she designed for Woods.

The inspiration for her patterns came largely from nature — **Bronze Chrysanthemums**, **Scarlet Runner Beans**, **A Country Bunch**, **Orchids**, and **Shepherd's Purse**.

Her incised ware featured squirrels, leaping deer, rams and goats, leaves and flowers. All were produced in subtle colours and with high or matt glazes. Her nursery ware often featured animals or illustrated nursery rhymes.

Her pottery sold at sensible prices, as she was aiming, as she said, at "professional people with taste and not much money".

At the British Industries Fair of 1932 Queen Mary bought a breakfast-in-bed set and a jug, and a buyer from John Lewis ordered her **Polka Dot** range. This was the beginning of a long and profitable association with the department store, which also involved the trying out of new lines and reporting back the buying public's response, giving Susie Cooper valuable market research.

In the same year she was elected to the North Staffordshire branch of the Council of the Society of Industrial Artists, often giving lectures at their meetings in support of her own ideas on pottery design.

By now Susie Cooper was supplying other department stores as well as John Lewis, among them Harrods, Waring and Gillow and Selfridges, and soon she realised that demand would outstrip supply unless she adopted additional new decorating techniques. She decided to introduce lithography in combination with hand-painting and aerographing. Lithography was just beginning to come forward with a wider palette of colours for mass manufacture, and Susie Cooper was to prove remarkably adept at making use of the innovations that were taking place.

By working closely with the manufacturers of lithographs, who were willing to use her own watercolour designs, she achieved a very high standard of lithography, resulting in designs like her famous **Dresden Spray**, a best-seller for nearly twenty years, **Iris**, **Clematis** and **Endon Border**, all of which had additional hand-painted decoration.

Similarly she was closely involved with all aspects of running her factory — staff recruitment and training (her workforce of five paintresses had increased to forty in two years) factory floor management and organisation, promotion and marketing — as well as producing up to two hundred patterns a year.

She advertised in the trade press and in top quality women's magazines, made appearances at annual trade fairs and had a showroom in London. This kept Susie Cooper's name in the forefront of pottery production throughout the Thirties, and by now she was exporting to Europe and Scandinavia, America and Canada, South Africa, Australia and New Zealand.

In 1939 the outbreak of war brought restrictions and shortages of material, but in 1940 Susie Cooper was made *Royal Designer for Industry*, the first woman in the Potteries to receive the award.

At first determined to carry on despite the problems of producing pottery in wartime, she was forced by a disastrous fire at Crown Works to cease production until rebuilding material became available in 1945, when she was able to resume.

In 1946 she was invited to join the selection committee for the *Britain Can Make It* exhibition at the Victoria and Albert Museum, three of her own designs being included.

At the British Industries Fair the following year her new designs included her popular **Tree of Life** pattern, and she was clearly re-established as a force to be reckoned with, but by now she had decided to branch out into china production and in 1950 she bought the Jason China Company of Longton.

A complete refit of the factory followed and 1951 saw the launch of a new shape, **Quail** for china. This was put on display in the Royal Pavilion at the Festival of Britain held at London's South Bank site.

Her post-war patterns, like those pre-war, drew their inspiration from nature and included *Teazle*, *Wild Strawberry*, *Sea Anemone* and *Whispering Grass*, while popular 1930s patterns continued to be made.

Sadly a tragic fire in 1957 halted production for nearly a year, but a merger with R. H. & S. L. Plant in 1961 gave Susie Cooper the opportunity to step up china production while phasing out earthenware, for which demand had declined.

When in 1966 Josiah Wedgwood and Sons Limited took over both the companies, Susie Cooper continued as a designer for the William Adams and Sons section of the Wedgwood empire.

Though at first regarding the change as a challenge, she eventually grew disillusioned by the impersonal nature of working in a huge organisation and many of her designs failed to reach the production stage. Although some new designs were sold in Boots and Tesco's in the early 1980s, this was not under her own name, and a far cry from acclaim she had enjoyed in earlier years.

A retrospective exhibition of her work under the title of *Elegance and Utility* was held by Wedgwood at the Sanderson's Exhibition Gallery in 1978, and in the New Year's Honours List of 1979 she received the OBE.

In October, 1982, the City Museum and Art Gallery at Hanley, Stoke-on-Trent, held an exhibition in tribute to her eightieth birthday, and in 1987 the Victoria and Albert Museum organised a travelling exhibition, *Susie Cooper Productions*.

In 1987 Wedgwood reintroduced three 1930s designs on the **Kestrel** shape, and in 1992 held an exhibition at their Visitors' Centre in tribute to her ninetieth birthday, including two room sets dressed with appropriate pottery.

Now resident with her son Timothy on the Isle of Man, Susie Cooper has produced seed paintings which have been successfully exhibited in London, designs for tapestry and felt appliqué cushions, and for her own celebration of her ninetieth birthday produced a limited edition of ninety of a model of a leaping deer, one of which was presented to the Queen Mother, who has been an admirer of Susie Cooper's work throughout her career.

Susie Cooper has obviously proved to be a dynamic and innovative designer throughout a large part of the twentieth century, and as such her contribution to the status of British pottery worldwide cannot be over-estimated. She has been an international celebrity, both before World War Two and since, and will be captivating collectors of her work for many more years to come.

SVC/Wedgwood 'Applegay' No. C2018, circa 1964

Quail shape 'One O'Clocks' coffee pot and Haw water No. 613, circa 1956

'Whispering Grass' toast and condiments, No. c609, produced circa 1956.

PATTERN NAMES

Since Susie Cooper is said to have designed more than 4500 patterns, it would be a mammoth task to get to know them all.

Probably the best method of getting familiar with her work is to pinpoint certain patterns or groups of patterns as being characteristic of a period in her career. Then unfamiliar patterns can be 'matched' to known patterns and an informed guess made as to their probable date. This is particularly useful when the backstamp is one used over a long period, for instance, a signature used from 1929 to 1980 or the familiar leaping deer used from 1932 to 1965.

Much of Susie Cooper's inspiration came from nature. Apart from geometric or 'cubist' patterns, banded designs and nursery ware, many of her patterns have floral names.

Sometimes the pattern name is shown by a lithograph on the base of the item. More usually a pattern number has been freehand painted into the box provided as part of the backstamp. In this case, the pattern and date can be identified by reference to a list based on the firm's pattern books or in the case of earlier work from the list of 'Pattern Numbers and Estimated Dates' given in *Hand-Painted Gray's Pottery* by Paul Niblett.

Advertising material and reviews of the annual trade fairs in the *Pottery Gazette and Glass Trades Review*, available at the Stoke-on-Trent City Library Reference Department, are also invaluable in providing information about pattern names and dates.

In some instances, in order to provide a ready means of identification, some familiar patterns originally known only by numbers have been given modern invented names by which they have become known to collectors. These by now have sometimes been adopted so thoroughly that it is difficult to remember that they are not original names. **Moon and Mountains**, for instance, brings brightly coloured circles and jagged lines to mind much more readily than the anonymous '7960'. It seems pedantic to object to this since it is so useful, especially to new collectors.

An additional guide is the complexity of the pattern, since Susie

Cooper naturally took into account the developing skills of her paintresses, being well aware from her own experience on piece work of the importance of keeping the pattern's demands within the capacity of the paintress while at the same time providing interest and variety in the manipulation of the brushstroke.

Initially Susie Cooper had been employed at Gray's Pottery as part of the team painting the range of lustre ware items designed by Gordon Forsyth. These were shown at the British Industries Fair in February, 1923. Soon afterwards she herself contributed as a designer to the Victoria and Albert Museum's exhibition *British Institute of Industrial Art, Recent Examples of British Pottery* held in September and October of that year. Around this time a special backstamp, incorporating her name, began to be used on her designs, which included brightly coloured floral and fruit patterns.

During the following years, Susie Cooper herself contributed designs to the Gloria Lustre range, usually identified by her monogram, a selection of which is shown in *Susie Cooper Productions* by Ann Eatwell. These pieces featured birds, animals and flowers, including goats, antelopes, lions and cherubs, and some were exhibited at the Wembley Exhibition of 1924 and at the Exposition des Arts Décoratifs in Paris in 1925.

As well as handpainted flower and fruit designs, the print and enamel technique was used over the next few years for patterns like **Acorns**, **Golden Catkin**, **Primula** and **Iris**. Nursery ware was not neglected, **Quadrupeds** appearing in a variety of colourways, featuring giraffes and gazelles as well as farmyard animals, while 'This is the House that Jack Built' and other children's motifs proved popular.

An important development in 1928 was her introduction of banding which she now used in both vivid and subtle combinations of colours.

By now geometric designs like **Moon and Mountains**, (black, red, yellow, green and blue circles and zigzags) and the 1929 **Cubist**, black, red, yellow, green, blue and grey blocks of colour, vied with the floral print and enamel patterns featuring crocuses and daffodils, and various banded patterns, including the attractive **Layebands** produced for Heals and named after the West End actress, Evelyn Laye, softly banded in yellow, pink and green.

Susie Cooper's time at Gray's ended with more floral and fruit patterns in bright colours, sometimes with gilt embellishment and sometimes with touches of lustre. **Summertime**, probably her last pattern for Gray's, summed up her work there with colourful flowers handpainted and edged with gilt.

Despite the uncertainty and insecurity of the George Street/Chelsea Works period, 1930-31, Susie Cooper's invention was unflagging. **Bronze Chrysanthemums** was her first recorded independent pattern, followed by a bouquet of floral patterns including **Carnation, Tulips, Lily of the Valley, Bluebell** and **Marigold**. Geometric and abstract designs punctuated the floral patterns, and spots began to appear, as in **Symphony**. Small stylised motifs like **Peacock Feathers**, in green, yellow and black, were introduced along with the black and red **Rose** and **Citrons** in orange, lemon, green and black, while **Deer Leap** foreshadowed a trademark yet to come.

The security of being established at Crown Works in 1931 led to a run of lively patterns; **Scarlet Runner Beans**, vivid in orange, red brown, black, yellow and hair brown, and **Tadpoles** green, orange, brown, grey and black, with **Galaxy** in yellow, blue, grey and black, as well as various abstract, geometric and floral designs and nursery ware like **Rabbit**.

The following year showed growing confidence both in her own administrative ability and in the skills of her paintresses, resulting in "**Panorama**", a charabanc on a trip to the country, **Caravan**, showing a man leading a horse-drawn caravan, and a variety of characters and animals such as **Balloon Man, Spanish Dancer, Clown, Woodpecker, Stag, Tigers, Squirrel** and **Monkey**.

Floral patterns continued, including **Briar Rose, Heliotrope, Cactus** and **Oak Apple**, a wide range of techniques — freehand painting, print and enamel, on-glaze and underglaze — being employed.

The year ended with Susie Cooper's development of wash-banding for one of her most popular patterns of all time, **Wedding Ring**, produced in many variations both pre-war and post-war.

In 1933 stylisation continued with **Leaf Pattern**, orange, yellow, blue, green and brown, **Florida** in pink, red, grey, black and green, and **Convulvulus**, blue, green, pink and amber, while abstract motifs like

Spiky Circle, **Blue Scrolls**, **Swirls**, brown and black and **Scrolls**, blue and black, became popular, with tube-lining being used for **Whirl**, **Swirl** and **Dropped Lines**. Floral patterns — **Country Flowers** in blue, green, yellow and purple, **Morello,** blue, orange, yellow and green, and **Gilley Flower**, blue green, purple, brown and black — remained an abiding theme, while **Playing Card Motifs**, **Diamonds**, **Hearts** and **Club** were an innovation.

In 1934 the success story of the year came near its end, with the use of thin sticks of marking colour utilised for underglaze painting. This was cleverly developed over the next few years in various ways — **Crayon Line** and **Crayon Swirl** in 1934, and **Crayon Loops** and **Crayon Scallop Border** in 1936, along with many crayon/banding variations. Two new patterns, **Egyptian** in blue, brown and black and **Pyramids** in red, brown and black, introduced motifs from Egypt, while new tube-lined patterns were put into production, including **Oak** and several unnamed designs. Aerographing was also used, sometimes in combination with sgraffito decoration, as in **Circles**.

By now Susie Cooper needed to speed up production to supply the increasing demand for her pottery, and in 1935 she began to introduce lithographs, designed by herself and specially produced for her to a very high standard. A variation on the print and enamel technique, it was much quicker in application and proved to be a success both commercially and aesthetically. **Dresden Spray** was enormously popular both pre- and post-war, retaining its popularity with today's collectors, while **Nosegay** and **Swansea Spray** were also best sellers.

With **Wedding Ring**, **Dresden Spray** and the crayon patterns as basic lines, Susie Cooper was now well-established, but she remained as versatile as ever, adding new floral patterns like **Blue Primula** and **Wide Buttercups** (1936) and **Faenza**, a green pattern of stylised feathers and dots, and **Exclamation Mark** while **Grey Leaf** appeared in various colourways, as did **Printemps**. Nursery animals like **Noah's Ark**, **Black Pom** and **Tango Terrier, Dignity and Impudence** were matched by **Golfer, Skier** and **Horse and Jockey** for the adults.

Two more popular lithographed patterns arrived in 1938, **Endon**, a delicate border pattern in green, pink and brown, and **Patricia Rose** in similar colours. Other patterns, like **Regency Feather** and **Elderberry**, combined aerographing with sgraffito. **Starbursts** made use of a star motif while **Sea Anemone** was a stylised transfer print of ferns in green, pink, orange and brown. The following year a fruit theme was introduced again — **Leaf and Vine**, **Apples and Pears**, **Pears and Cherries**, **Pear and Plum** and **Grapevine**, often with turquoise predominant, followed by more feather, star and circle motifs. **Long Leaf** in green, yellow and pink, was another popular transfer pattern.

The outbreak of war led to a shortage of materials and manpower, but **Black Leaves** was introduced early in 1940 and proved popular. The following year, old favourites continued in production, backed up by new patterns like **Tulip** and **Daisy Spray**, **Pink Aster Spray** and **Tigerlily**.

Bud, mainly pinks and greens, and **Seaweed** were introduced in 1942 but early that year a disastrous fire ended production until after the war.

As to be expected, there was a complete change in public taste once the war was over, and Susie Cooper was swift to respond to the new demand despite continuing shortages of labour and materials. Deprived temporarily of the option of lithography, due to the fire which destroyed all her stocks, she returned to banding, freehand painting and sgraffito for striking patterns like **Tree of Life** and **Tulip in Pompadour**, often using deeper colours like green, brown and mahogany to suit contemporary interiors.

Following the move into china production in 1950, lithography once again became central as a decorating technique and floral patterns like **Gardenia**, **Magnolia**, **Orchid** and **Azalea** joined **Blue Star**, **Gold Bud** and **Astral**.

Classical designs like **Corinthian**, **Romanesque** and **Palladian** were offered along with **Highland Grass**, **Sienna Pastel** and **Pomme D'or**, providing a wide range of options for the customer.

Two years after the second fire in 1957, Susie Cooper purchased the Crown Works and from then on earthenware was gradually phased out, until by 1964 she had switched over entirely to bone china. Once again Susie Cooper fell victim to fire, and her lithography gave way to hand-painting and sgraffito, with **Black Fruit**, **Confetti** and **Relief Polka Dot** using aerographed decoration.

Amalgamation with R. H. and S. L. Plant Ltd led to further china ware development and after new floral patterns like **Cornflower, Speedwell, Wild Rose** and **Glen Mist** in blues and greys, Susie Cooper began to explore the covercoat technique which was beginning to oust both lithography and hand-painting. Covercoat, or 'slide', was simpler in application and gave a much more uniform density of colour. It was, ideal for the intense modern colours appropriate to the Swinging Sixties. Silk-screened on to film, the pattern slid off on to the ware cleanly and easily, giving consistently perfect results for the minimum of effort.

Christmas Rose and **White Jasmine** were early covercoat patterns, but perhaps better known were those after March 1966, the time of the Wedgwood takeover, like **Carnaby Daisy, Diablo** in gold and black, and the best-selling **Corn Poppy**, red, brown and black on white.

As well as tableware, Susie Cooper designed giftware for Wedgwood, **Floral Bouquet** for the Silver Jubilee, the **English Wild Flower** series and **Birds of the World**.

In 1982, following the final closure of the Crown Works in 1980 and working from a studio at William Adams and Sons Ltd, at Tunstall, Susie Cooper designed **Blue Daisy, Meadowlands** and **Inspiration** to be sold in chain stores, her final design being a new covercoat version of **Florida** in 1984.

Apart from a revival of three 1930s patterns, **Marguerite, Pink Fern** and **Polka Dot** in time for the 1987 Victoria and Albert Museum exhibition of her work, Wedgwood produced no new Susie Cooper patterns from 1984, though for her ninetieth birthday she created, appropriately enough, a limited edition of ninety leaping deer in porcelain.

DECORATING TECHNIQUES

Susie Cooper's early experiences in the decorating shop at Gray's Pottery gave her in-depth knowledge. She was aware of the necessity for the decoration and the technique by which it was applied to be in harmony with each other and to be within the capabilities of the decorator.

Just as Clarice Cliff designed bold geometric patterns for her young apprentices to apply to the stocks of dated whiteware she had been given for her early experiments, so Susie Cooper at first restricted her designs to simple banding, blocks of colour, spots, stars and stylised flowers.

Then, as her skills increased, she designed patterns using more complicated brushwork and techniques until the paintresses were capable of a whole range of variations and could reproduce at speed any of the many hundreds of patterns she designed, using any method specified.

Susie Cooper joined Gray's at the point when Gordon Forsyth was designing a lustre ware range. This, intended to be launched under the range name of 'Gloria Lustre', employed various metallic glazes and featured heraldic birds and beasts, flowers and fruit.

Difficult to apply and fugitive in wear, *lustre painting* uses metals like gold, silver, titanium, platinum and bronze in compounds which are painted on over the glaze and the fired in a reducing or oxygen-starved atmosphere in order to leave a thin film on the surface of the ware, either giving a solid metallic colour or an iridescent effect. It is a technique more suited to decorative objects than those intended for daily use, and requires perfect preparation and firing conditions for success. Susie Cooper helped in the production of Gordon Forsyth's designs, usually being responsible for painting the heraldic lions which were a prominent symbol in the range.

Also at Gray's Susie Cooper developed a wide variety of *banding* and *lining* techniques used in different combinations of width and strength. The bands of colour could be solid, shaded or washed on using colour mixed with turps or aniseed to make it flow evenly.

Another technique she was later to use in her own factory was the *print and enamel* method, whereby a printed outline was applied to the surface of the ware and then colour applied to enhance the decoration. This method, speedier than total hand-painting, was in wide use throughout the Potteries.

On-glaze decoration was also widely used, the paint being applied after the piece had been glazed, using enamel colours, then fired at a low temperature.

Under-glaze decoration, like the **Crayon** patterns were carried out freehand with sticks of colour made up specially for Susie Cooper. They were applied on the biscuit (i.e. unglazed) ware and glazed afterwards, giving a depth and richness to the finished result.

Tube-lining — outlining the pattern with liquid slip extruded from the glass nozzle of a rubber bag — was another technique carried out before glazing, considerable experience being required to ensure the surface was neither too wet nor too dry for the thin thread of clay to adhere. Charlotte Rhead is the ceramic artist best known for her tube-lined designs, and the technique has also been in constant use at the Moorcroft factory where it remains so to this day, but Susie Cooper also produced some very stylish tube-lined designs, including **Dropped Line**, spiral effects and floral patterns outlined in tubing.

A combination of under- and on-glaze decoration known as *in-glaze* was achieved by painting on glaze with underglaze colour and letting the colour melt when fired, to create a three-dimensional effect.

In some instances, simple patterns were applied freehand, but for more complicated patterns a *pounce* was used, a pierced outline of the patterns through which charcoal dust was blown to provide guidelines. Sometimes these were overdrawn with Indian ink. The ink and charcoal vanished when the item was fired.

Very typical of Susie Cooper's style of decoration was the *Incised* ware in which the decoration (flowers, leaves, squirrels, deer, goats and stags) was carved into the leather-hard clay body before glazing, often with a matt glaze, and firing.

Similarly, in *Sgraffito* decoration the piece was first glazed in a solid colour and the pattern incised freehand through the glaze. Increasing commercial pressure led to the use of aerographing, (the use of a spray gun), for shading borders and to prepare pieces for Sgraffito decoration.

Lithography was also used to speed up production as demand increased. A form of transfer printing, it had been widely used but as the designs were often created by artists not familiar with pottery production the results were frequently less than satisfactory. Unwilling to accept this, Susie Cooper worked to create a co-operative relationship with the manufacturers and persuaded them to produce lithographs from her own water-colours so that a high standard of suitability was possible. She was to have many successes with this method, including **Dresden Spray**, **Printemps**, **Cactus** and **Nosegay**.

After the war, *silk-screen* techniques replaced lithography to a large extent since there was now a demand for more permanent colours due to the advent of detergents and dish-washers. A screen being used for each colour, the pattern was built up on to the film from which it was then applied to the pottery and the backing sheet removed. This also is known as the 'covercoat' method.

SVC 'Diablo' No. c2150, circa 1969.

Beakers for World Wildlife Fund, No c2203, about 1970

'Silver Jubilee' limited editions of 500 c2208, circa 1977/78.

'Venetia' coffee pot c2039, produced circa 1964.

'Hyde Park' coffee pot No. c192, produced circa 1959.

SHAPES

During her time at Gray's, Susie Cooper had very little opportunity to design shapes and this was a major reason for her dissatisfaction, leading to her determination to set up her own factory.

At Gray's she did, however, design the shape of a *coffee-pot* which was produced for Gray's by Johnson Brothers Ltd. It was made in about 1928 and was 20cm high. Probably around the same time she designed a *teapot, milk jug* and *sugar bowl* which were produced for Gray's by Lancaster and Sons Ltd.

Once the Susie Cooper Pottery was safely established at the Crown Works, Burslem in the summer of 1931, she was able to design shapes to be made for her by the adjacent factory of Wood and Sons, and as a result the *Kestrel* shape appeared at the *British Industries Fair* in 1932.

The following year the *Curlew* shape was shown at the same event, as well as the *Kestrel* tureen with its reversible lid.

Susie Cooper also designed shapes for Wood and Sons. The *Wren* shape for them appeared in 1935, and was followed by *Jay*. She modified their *Classic* and *Rex* shapes and from 1935 used these for her own patterns as well. In 1937 the *Falcon* shape was launched, and the following year's B.I.F. saw the *Spiral* shape unveiled.

Despite changing tastes post-war, Susie Cooper's shapes remained popular, especially decorated with her new patterns designed to appeal to current taste. As she moved into china in 1950 she designed the *Quail* shape for the 1951 Festival of Britain.

Following the fire of 1957 the *Can* shape proved popular and was to remain so until 1989, while the *Fluted* shape, designed in 1956 but not shown until the following year, was also a success. Also in 1957 the *Scallop* shape was designed and shown at the Blackpool Fair.

After the move to William Adams in Tunstall the *Simple* shape was also effective with Susie Cooper patterns of the 1980s, as was the *Hexagon* shape, both being made by Adams.

Finally, the wheel came full circle when in 1987-8 Wedgwood issued three Susie Cooper designs from the 1930s on *Kestrel* shape breakfast sets, issued in presentation boxes.

'Papyrus' or 'Thebes' production samples circa 1974/75

Fluted shape boxed set No c875 circa 1958.

26

BACKSTAMPS AND OTHER METHODS OF DATING

So recognisable is Susie Cooper's work that it is often unnecessary to turn an item over to check the backstamp on the base.

With experience, a collector will also soon be able to hazard a fairly accurate guess as to the period of her career to which it belongs, judging by the type of pattern and method of decoration.

Shape is also a guide to dating as the item clearly falls into the period in which that particular shape was in production.

Certain popular patterns were in production for long periods and will require other clues to pinpoint the probable date of production within that period. Some patterns were produced only briefly or only in small quantities, and in these cases there is less latitude for error.

Where a designer moved from one factory to another, as Susie Cooper did from Gray's Pottery to her own factory, it must be remembered that certain of her patterns were kept in production after she left, sometimes for a period of several years, and these will therefore carry the later backstamp, in this instance Gray's clipper backstamp.

Sometimes the backstamps incorporated the name of a pattern in the form of a lithograph, while occasionally a backstamp was designed especially for a particular pattern which it named as part of the backstamp design. This is obviously helpful, particularly if it is an unfamiliar pattern in production only briefly.

Dating pottery can never be an exact science as at the time it was made it was not anticipated that one day it would become collectable, so the application of backstamps was often haphazard and sometimes misleading.

Shape, pattern and backstamp are all useful clues to identifying items, but no more than clues. Best of all is hard evidence in the form of provenance — details from the original owner or the family of the original owner as to when it was bought, particularly in the case of a wedding gift, a twenty-first birthday present or an anniversary presentation.

Apart from such evidence, it is best not to be too dogmatic in attempting to date any particular piece. In the case of Susie Cooper, many backstamps were in use, sometimes simultaneously, for several years, even up to half a century, while certain popular patterns were in production for several decades.

Impressed marks on the base of some items indicate not the date of decoration but the date of the manufacture of the whiteware. Decoration was necessarily, therefore, after this date, but how long after is difficult to determine.

Pattern numbers, sometimes painted freehand in the box incorporated into certain backstamps, are a useful guide as they can be checked against the lists of Susie Cooper patterns based on the pattern books from which the paintresses worked, but again it is necessary to remember that patterns were often in production over a period of years. All that is indicated by the pattern number is that the piece was decorated between those two dates. The first is arbitrary (though it cannot have been decorated before the pattern was designed!) and the other, later date, is flexible to some extent as occasionally in the 1930s 'matchings' could be ordered by the customer to replace broken items in discontinued patterns.

An impressed mark beginning with a 'W' (for Woods) indicates the date of manufacture of the whiteware, the last two digits being the year and the prior digit(s) being the month of production.

The majority of patterns designed by Susie Cooper for Gray's carried a backstamp she had herself designed. Keeping to Gray's existing tradition of a theme of ships, she brought this up to date by creating a picture of a liner with two funnels using orange, green and black, with "Handpainted" above and the wording below reading "Gray's Pottery, Hanley. England. Designed by Susie Cooper". Used from 1923 to about 1931, by which time she had, of course, left the company, variations were evolved to cover Nursery ware, when the mark was in blue only, or sometimes reading simply 'Susie Cooper Ware'. Sometimes, printed in black only or brown, the backstamp included the name of the pattern. Occasionally it was used without the final line which read "Designed by Susie Cooper", presumably for work by other designers, or for items decorated after she left the factory.

Boxed Fruits, perhaps No. c899.

Her first independent mark was a simple triangle applied by a rubber stamp and therefore often a little blurred, since it was applied on top of the glaze. It read succinctly 'A Susie Cooper Production', sometimes with the additional wording 'Burslem, England'. Used from 1930 to 1932, it was stamped in black. It is said that a similar backstamp had been used previously at the George Street premises in the autumn of 1929, when the additional wording was, of course, 'Tunstall, England' instead of 'Burslem'.

Most familiar by far is the Leaping Deer backstamp, introduced in 1932 and used until the mid-sixties with a vast number of variations. The usual wording read 'A Susie Cooper Production, Crown Works, Burslem England' with a box below into which a pattern number could be painted freehand. Usually printed in brown, it was sometimes found in green or blue, with or without a pattern number or, from time to time, with a pattern name. Between 1932 and 1956 the wording only of this backstamp was occasionally used, without the deer. Sometimes, too, the deer and the box were missing, the box being replaced by a very neatly written script signature with a circle below the line that was inscribed beneath the name. Various incised signatures, some with dates or reference numbers, were used from 1932 to 1980, particularly on studio ware, England being added below on many items.

A variety of printed signatures was used from 1933 to the mid-sixties, usually in brown but sometimes in green. 'England' was often added from 1934. Again reference numbers or pattern names were occasionally added.

Some patterns, made for John Lewis and/or Peter Jones, the big department stores, were marked not with Susie Cooper's name but the the name of the retailer and the pattern name, and the pattern's predominant colour was then used for the backstamp.

A special Woods backstamp was used on items which carried patterns designed by Susie Cooper for Woods, sometimes also indicating 'Designed by Susie Cooper for Awmacks Leeds, manufactured by Wood and Sons Ltd'.

Bone china was at first marked with a delicate signature with an asterisk below and the words 'Bone China England' printed in brown, black, green or blue. This mark was used from 1950 to around 1966.

A circular backstamp printed in black and reading 'Susie Cooper Made in England' round the edge with 'Fine Bone China' in the centre, was used from about 1957 to 1960 and may have been intended for the export market, hence the emphasis on its English origins.

Another printed signature above 'Susie Cooper Fine Bone China England' followed, printed in black and sometimes with the pattern name and/or number, and from 1967, 'Member of the Wedgwood Group'.

Later marks sometimes included the Wedgwood Vase motif with or without the wording 'Susie Cooper Design' and other descriptive details.

From 1982, Adams' Crown trademark and name replaced any mention of Susie Cooper herself, though Wedgwood retained the words 'Susie Cooper Design' until the late 1980s.

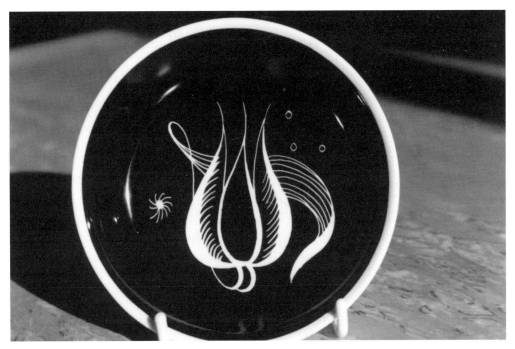

SVC sweet dish sgraffito decoration 'Orchid' perhaps c403, circa 1953.

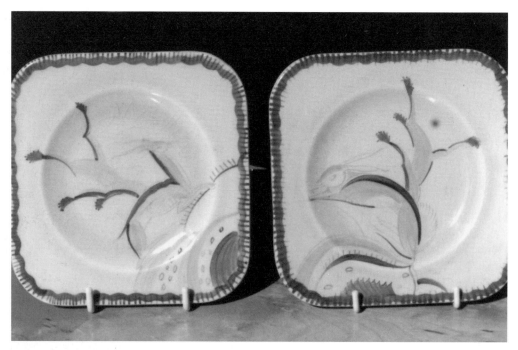

Gray's 'Pastoral' No. 8321, circa 1928.

Gray's 'Quadrupeds' No 7742, circa 1928.

Guan Yin — modelled in bone china by Susie Cooper when at the Burslem School of Art, and painted in enamel colours with gilt embellishment. This striking figure in oriental costume is one four produced between 1919-1922 and is 16.5cm high. The others are of a Flower Seller, a Spanish Lady and a powder bowl modelled as a crinoline lady holding a posy of flowers. (N Jones)

The shape of this coffee pot was designed by Susie Cooper while at Gray's and the vivid geometric pattern in green, black, yellow and grey is also her work. It was because there were few opportunities to design shapes at Gray's that Susie Cooper felt impelled to set up as an independent pottery producer and so embarked on a career that was to lead to international fame. (N Jones)

A fruit set in a bold handpainted floral pattern. (Courtesy Christies)

A Cube tea set, panels of overlapping rectangles and wavy lines handpainted in yellow, green, grey, brown, ochre and black, with the early triangular backstamp. (Courtesy Christies)

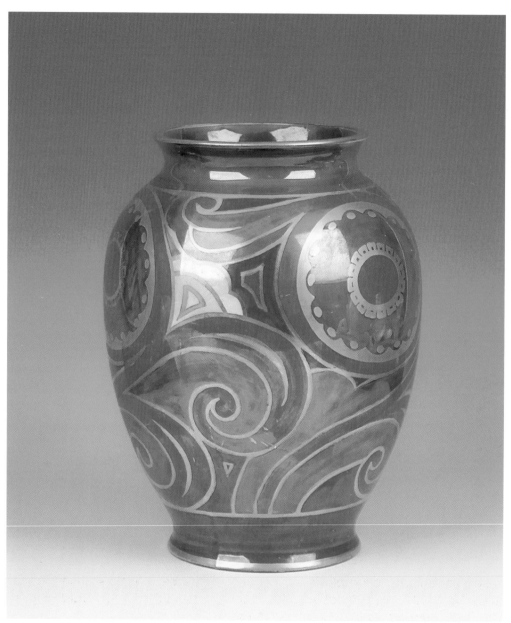

A Gloria Lustre ovoid vase with scalloped flower-heads enclosed in scrolled lines in lustre red and blue with gold embellishment, produced for Gray's (c1925). The Gloria Lustre range was initiated at Gray's by Gordon Forsyth, who was a major influence on Susie Cooper at this time. It carried a special backstamp, a sunray in black and yellow, and included ornamental and useful items, richly decorated in a variety of lustres. (NJ)

Three Gloria Lustre examples — a pear-shaped vase in gold on green and purple, a waisted cylindrical vase in pink, lilac and gilt and an ovoid vase in blue, pink, purple and gilt. (Courtesy Christies)

A Gray's part coffee service in silver lustre, showing shallows in flight, which was made for Heal's. (Courtesy Christies). Below (left) SVC Canadia export plate, circa 1950; (right) Gray's lustre jug, circa 1928.

Four late 1920s pieces for Gray's with a 1930s geometric design, middle left. (NJ)

Leaping Deer handpainted wall plaque.

Late 1930s Fox handpainted wall plaque.

The saucer of the moustache cup was decorated with barber's equipment "Dignity and Impudence", the two dogs, taking its title from a Victorian oil-painting by Landseer, is shown here on a Paris shape jug and dates from around 1936. It is transfer printed in orange, yellow and black with narrow blue and yellow bands, while the plate behind it shows Cowboy, from the same time.

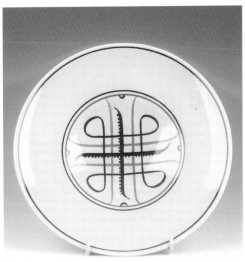

A sense of humour often enlivened her work — the moustache cup and saucer (c1933) was designed for the American market.

A plate dating from about 1933 showing the pattern shown at the Exhibition of British Art in that year. (NJ)

Another humorous design was **Golfer**, on a large breakfast cup, he looks down a hole, his club behind him.

The Cowboy and his horse appear again on this lamp-base, banded in orange and yellow. (NJ)

Susie Cooper never lost her love of modelling, and in the early 1930s produced several wall-masks — a Judge, a Chinaman and one based on film star Greta Garbo, and sold under the name of Brunette. A fourth, a stylised self-portrait of herself was not put into production.(N Jones)

Teaware items in a beautiful handpainted floral pattern. (Courtesy Christies)

An attractive mixture of Gray's and Crown Works coffee cans, a space-saving item to collect. (Courtesy Christies)

While at Gray's, Susie Cooper designed a number of striking geometric patterns, including the one known to collectors as **Moon and Mountains** which is shown on the two plates here and **Cubist** shown on the vase and the large jug on the right. Unfortunately, such large areas of flat colour tended to flake and though she also produced some geometric patterns in the early years of her own factory, they were eventually discontinued. (N Jones)

A geometric vase with an unusual shape and pattern in blue, yellow, grey, black and white enamels. (NJ)

A superb geometric globular vase in subtle shades of brown, yellow, black and grey on cream. (Beverley's)

The strongly defined brushwork and brilliant colours gave this geometric square plate more impact.

A geometric bowl in greens, yellow, orange and black. Again strong brushwork led to greater impact. (NJ)

A **Kestrel** coffee service in geometric patterning (top) and another in a very unusual abstract design featuring rectangles, dots and angular black lines. (Courtesy Christies)

A coffee set. The rather elaborate shape is from the early years of Susie Cooper's factory, c1932-1934. (NJ)

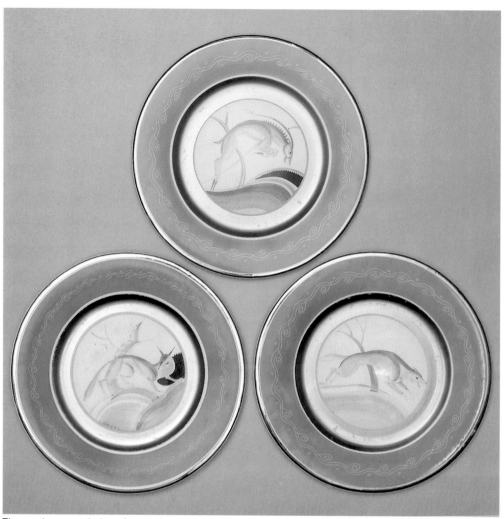

Three large plates from the mid-1930s featuring animal subjects, with sgraffito decoration. (Courtesy Christies)

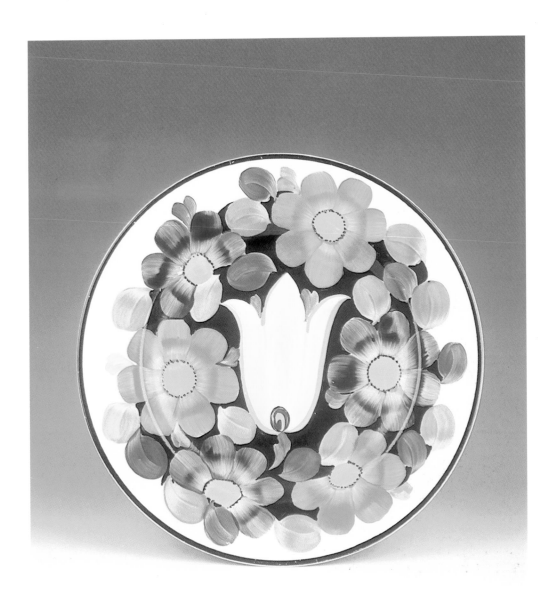

An earthenware floral plate with a pattern designed by Susie Cooper towards the end of her time at Gray's (c1928). Painted in red, blue, orange, green, yellow and black, it had a yellow glaze and was used on tableware, featuring a large bell-shaped central flower surrounded by seven-petalled red and blue flowers and circular green leaves. (Beverley)

Aerographing with sgraffito decoration was a technique which Susie Cooper developed and used throughout her career. On the blue-green plates it is used as a border, with spiral embellishment to the centre, and on the trio ribbon decoration has been used to give lightness and delicacy to the deep colour, in combination with a single narrow band. (NJ)

On these large plates, the central area is decorated with fish, birds or animals and the rim has a simple pattern of lines and dots. (NJ)

Inspiration from nature always remained the mainspring of her work, as these show, the Turkey plates being designed for Thanksgiving celebrations. The **Leaping Deer**, of course, was also incorporated in the trademark she used for over 30 years. (NJ)

The **Woodpecker**, shown here on items from a dinner service, was a print and enamel pattern from 1932, in yellow, green, black and grey, banded in grey with an edge of pink spots. (Courtesy Christies)

A very unusual, highly decorated wall-plate, featuring strongly stylised flowers and a bowl of fruit. (Courtesy Christies)

A Gray's plate in orange, red, black and yellow in a geometric pattern with a Crown Works triangular galleon lamp base, a Seafull biscuit barrel and a Gloria Lustre ginger jar. (Courtesy Christies)

A batchelor set, *Kestrel* shape, deep blue with crescent sgraffito, made at the Crown Works. (Courtesy Christies)

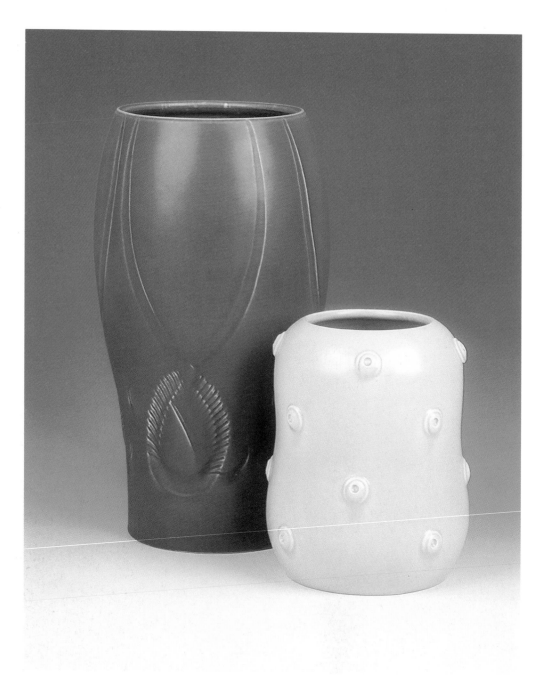

Another studio ware vase, this time with an abstract pattern incised, 30.7cm high and dating from about 1936, with a smaller white vase, decorated with self-coloured buttons. A large range of this ware was produced in many strong colours, including blues, pinks, greens, yellows, cream, white and even red. (N J)

This table centre with a leaping deer, painted in fawn, brown and green with a matching flower-trough in three parts, was also made in the mid-1930s and sometimes had a matching model of a pursuing hound. (NJ)

In her incised ware, too, Susie Cooper chose animals for subjects. Here a grey-green jug is decorated with leaping rams, and a large pink vase with squirrels, both from around 1933, while the small matt-glazed vase has a pattern of leaves and buds. (NJ)

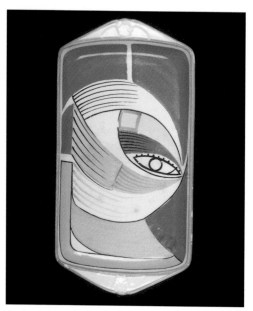

A very unusual handpainted tray in strong colours with an 'eye' motif. (Courtesy Christies)

A charger with a central leaf motif, banded in grey and ochre. (Courtesy Christies)

Bone china cups and saucers featuring interior decoration and gilt handles from the early 1950s, including the **Orchid** and **Tulip** patterns. (Courtesy Christies)

A box and lid decorated with the **Scarlet Runner Beans** pattern (1931), painted in yellow, orange, black and brown with matching banding. This lively pattern was typical of this period of her work. (NJ)

Two floral teaware patterns from the same time, hand-painted in strong colours. (NJ)

Early floral patterns, all hand-painted, and a beaker in **The Homestead**, one of a number of patterns designed to be produced in small quantities. This, a rare example of a landscape pattern, echoes the Clarice Cliff cottages going into production around this time. (NJ)

A **Kestrel** shape *Tea for Two* with pink scalloped edging and pink motifs. The **Kestrel** shape appeared at the British Industries Fair in 1932. It was an instant success and remains perhaps her most popular shape. (NJ)

The *Two Leaf Spray* pattern of 1935, with green interiors and dotted edge, also in the **Kestrel** shape. (NJ)

A pale blue Breakfast set in the **Kestrel** shape, including a muffin dish with a double-walled base to hold hot water, to keep toast or muffins warm, and with a lidded hot water jug.

An Asterix coffee set, this time in the **Falcon** shape from 1937. *Asterix* was one of Susie Cooper's most successful patterns, begun in 1934. This shape was not made for John Lewis though. (NJ)

Graduated black bands and tango orange decorate this striking **Kestrel** shape teaset, dating from about 1932. Other colours were used in combination with the graduated black bands, including blue, pale green and yellow. (NJ)

Maximising on the skill of her banders, Susie Cooper went on to develop this theme, using several colours in bands and adding, as herewith dots and crosses as variations. (NJ)

Another **Kestrel** coffee set, this time in a subtle combination of pink and brown with dots and crosses, the decoration of the pot being on the upper section. (NJ)

A **Kestrel** coffee set, this time in yellow with black, the decoration emphasising the elegant shape of the pot. (NJ)

A large service plate, the central motif of the antelope in brown, grey and yellow, with banding in the same colours and a dotted edge. One of a series of similar plates with animals as their subject from the mid-1930s it is an example of Susie Cooper's vigorous yet economical drawing of natural subjects. (NJ)

Due to commercial pressure, Susie Cooper enterprisingly turned to lithographs based on her own watercolours. **Dresden Spray** (1935) was to prove her most popular pattern, in production to the end of the 1950s. (N J)

Skilfully adapted to fit all shapes and sizes of ware and banded in a wide vareity of colours, it has retained its popularity with today's collectors. (NJ)

These examples, from a charger to a coaster, show how effectively the basic lithograph could be made to fit perfectly any size or shape. The borders were added by hand, and the pattern became Susie Cooper's best-seller, analogous to Clarice Cliff's Crocus. (NJ)

Even egg-cups got the Dresden Spray treatment, while another very popular pattern was **Printemps**, of 1936, made up of the previous year's lithograph, **Swansea Spray**, but with a decorative scalloped border added. (NJ)

Like Desden Spray, **Printemps** was versatile, decorating here a double jamdish. The salad dish is in **Charcoal Feather**, a post-war pattern. (NJ)

Swansea Spray is shown here on the trio in the foreground, and on the right-hand plate with decorative motifs on the border. The right-hand centre cup and saucer is in **Printemps**, the **Kestrel** teapot shows another very popular pattern, **Long Leaf**, and the plate on the left is a later bone-china example.

Here the trios are different colourways of **Grey Leaf** and the large jug has the **Nosegay** pattern. The cups and saucers are in **Gardenia** and a feather pattern.

Teaware on the left, in the **Endon** pattern (c1938), in the *Spiral* shape of the same year, was printed in pink, green and sepia, while the teacup and saucer in **Long Leaf** (1939), has banding in pink and green. (NJ)

In about 1940, **Patricia Rose** made its appearance, attactively coloured in pink, yellow, brown and green. Banded usually in pink, grey or blue, it here has an attractively scalloped border in pink with dots. (NJ)

Gardenia, from the early 1950s, was another very attractive floral pattern, seen here on a coffee set banded in two shades of green. The **Kestrel** shape was still very popular at this time. (NJ)

Various teawares, Ferndown jug and basin (c1959) a wildflower pattern trio, a banded trio in pink and brown and a dotted teapot in the *Falcon* shape. (NJ)

The *Falcon* shape again, this time for a cord and ring transfer print, "Elegance", the lid of the coffee pot, the rims and interiors of the jug and basin handpainted in blue. (NJ)

Fruit motifs were popular in the 1950s on both china and earthenware. Here, a plate in a fruit pattern and a cup and saucer in berry design. (NJ)

A dividend nursery plate with a pig, a **Horse and Jockey** plate, another dividend plate with a cow, a **Skier** cocoa pot, a lampbase with a duck, a **Dignity and Impudence** mug and a **Quadrupeds** sugar bowl. (Courtesy Christies)

A Crown Works vegetable tureen on a matching stand and ladle in **Crayon Loop**. (Courtesy Christies)

Three teaplates in various shapes — including **Acorn**, a popular pattern for many years. (NJ)

Three floral patterns, including **Tigerlily**, the motif in red, pink and green. (NJ)

An early geometric coffee cup and a small bowl in Hazelwood (c1959) with a central motif of hazel nuts and leaves, banded in brown.

A Gray's tableware pattern, a central motif in blue, green and yellow, with a dotted blue edge and yellow banding.

A tureen and stand from a Gray's part dinner service featuring a floral motif and a yellow dotted border. (Courtesy Christies)

A Kestrel tureen and oval platter, the tureen in **Pear in Pompadour** and the platter in **Tulip in Pompadour**. (Courtesy Christies)

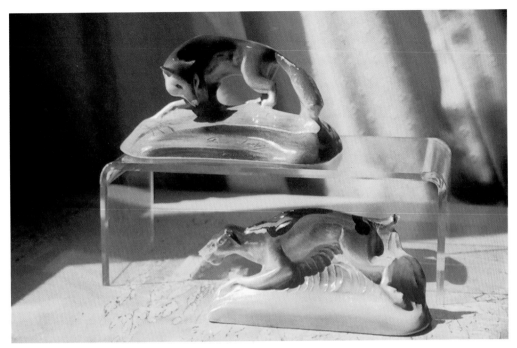

SVC Fox and Hound circa 1934

`Ashmun' motif No. c2206 circa 1974/75.

Fruit and vegetable depicted on a plate in pink, green, ochre and brown with scrolled banding. (Courtesy Christies)

A 'Tree of Life' plate and an 'Apples' plate. (Courtesy Christies)

Two Gloria Lustre pieces — a 1924 footed bowl decorated with a goat and a ginger jar with a ram motif. (Courtesy Christies)

Items from every stage of Susie Cooper's pre-war career.

NOTES FOR COLLECTORS

Starting a Susie Cooper Collection

Often a collection is started almost by accident, when one or more items are inherited from a relative, and in this case those first items may dictate the direction the collection is to take. Additional items may be purchased to 'go with' the first pieces and the collection will grow by means of gifts and further purchases till it becomes an absorbing hobby.

Eventually it may even become a spare time occupation, as the need to sell off surplus items to raise funds to buy more suitable ones leads into occasional dealing at antique fairs, perhaps, with retirement, becoming a full-time occupation and lifelong interest.

For collectors this new found interest adds purpose to weekend outings, with planned visits to antique fairs and holidays offering new antique venues to explore with the collection in mind.

Some collectors like to collect 'across the board', buying what takes their fancy out of what comes their way and including examples from all periods of Susie Cooper's career, while others prefer to specialise in one or more periods or even select a favourite pattern, perhaps to fill a dresser or a particular set of shelves.

Alternatively, 'shape' can be the deciding factor, for example, coffee cans, which look attractive as a group, or wall-plates which will form a decorative display on almost any wall of the house.

Some collectors aim at getting a single example of each pattern, but since it has been estimated that Susie Cooper designed around 4500 patterns, this is a mammoth task.

Others decide to build up 'sets', which can be done piece by piece, though it is important to ensure that the condition of each piece is consistent throughout. It is important, too, that the pieces in the collection harmonise with their setting. One way to ensure this is to emulate the original buyers, and to choose pieces with a particular setting in mind. Vases and tablelamps, for instance, are particularly suitable for sitting-rooms or bedrooms, while nursery ware displays attractively in the kitchen or bathroom.

'Trios' (a single cup, saucer and plate) will display well and do not demand a large outlay, while at the same time they allow a wide range of patterns to be shown.

When more funds are available, teapots look impressive, especially if accompanied by a matching hot water jug and perhaps milk jug and sugar basin. Complete teasets are less practical, taking up as they do so much more room.

Bread and Butter Plates, being slightly 'dished' rather than the flat shape of dinner or pudding plates, are particularly effective either on the wall or behind a small group of matching items.

Very small items, like cruets, toastracks, egg-cups, ash-trays and candlesticks make an interesting collection and are easily accommodated, but unfortunately in these cases price seldom relates to size and they can be expensive. Another factor is that collecting these items brings the Susie Cooper collector into competition with egg-cup collectors, toast-rack collectors and so on.

Since at present, pre-war Susie Cooper shapes and patterns are the most collectable, and therefore the most expensive, if funds are limited, collectors with an eye to the future will not neglect post-war patterns, many of which are typical of their own period and as such are likely to be very sought after in years to come, with the added advantage that they can be found now at very reasonable prices, sometimes even in charity shops or at flea markets. It is worth bearing in mind that some of the best collections in the country were built up from similar humble sources in the days before Susie Cooper pottery was thought of as being not only collectable but of vast investment potential.

To accompany a collection, it is interesting to build up a scrap-book of cuttings, articles and information about Susie Cooper, which can be stored in a folder with transparent display sleeves. This will add enjoyment to the collection while at the same time providing valuable reference material for pattern identification and dating.

Record keeping

Almost certainly as time goes by, a collector will find that certain pieces in his collection no longer fit the parameters he has set himself and he will want to part with them. This is where record-keeping comes into its own.

If the pieces have come to him as gifts, he will of course probably have little idea what was paid for them or where they were bought, but if they are items he has bought himself, his records will be invaluable in reminding him of the transactions involved.

This is why it is essential, from the very start of a collection, to keep a careful note of each item. Polaroid photographs, too, are helpful not only as a visual record of the collection to refer to when adding to it away from home, but also for insurance purposes.

The date of each purchase should be noted, with its cost (plus a note too of the asking price if what has been paid is a price agreed between seller and purchaser) details of the seller and some brief details of shape, pattern and condition, especially any distinguishing marks by which it would be recognisable in case of theft. The details on the base should either be written down or photographed. Backstamps are particularly important if a set is being collected as matching backstamps, though not essential, are desirable in most cases.

With complete records, it is much easier to approach a dealer with a view to selling or perhaps part-exchanging items which are no longer suitable for the collection. Inevitably as knowledge and appreciation grows, standards rise and what was considered acceptable in the early haphazard days of collecting is now inappropriate for inclusion with more recent and carefully considered acquisitions.

As well as practical considerations, there is also the satisfaction to be gained from monitoring the rising prices of Susie Cooper pottery. Already her work is offered for sale at specialist auctions in London and commands prices which would have seemed exaggerated even just a few years ago. As with Clarice Cliff, certain designs are attracting particularly high prices at present, and as these special items get more scarce, patterns now thought to be run-of-the-mill will shortly be in much greater demand. Though collectors value their items primarily for the outstanding talent which has gone into their making, the investment potential exists and is a further justification for all the dedication and hard work that goes into making a collection of this kind.

Insurance

Once a collection really gets under way, considerations of insurance naturally arise, since all too soon the aggregate value of the pottery puts it outside the scope of ordinary household insurance.

Particularly if one or more individual items of are high value, it is best to check if they exceed the top limit of existing insurance. If so, separate insurance is going to be required.

This will need updating at regular intervals since as prices rise replacement costs rise with them.

If the collection contains, say, a coffee set or a tea for two, this fact must be pointed out when insurance is discussed, as the loss of a single item such as a cup or milk jug, would ruin the whole set, being perhaps in some cases impossible to replace, yet unless this matter has been taken into account, insurance liability may be for the single broken item only.

The cost of insuring a collection is in proportion to the total value of the pieces, and as most people have already taken precautions against burglary in their routine insurance situation, this cover extends to the separate insurance of the collection. It is in any case unlikely that except in the case of a targeted theft, ordinary intruders would try to carry off fragile pottery. Accidental damage is more likely to be the cause of a claim.

Making a claim is much easier when careful records have been kept, and 'before' and 'after' photographs give positive proof that damage has occurred. Many insurance companies also require one or more statements from reputable antique dealers that the item was worth what the collector claims and will cost this sum to replace.

Sometimes, in the case of an irreplaceable item, the collector will wish to consider restoration and estimates for this must be submitted, bearing in mind the loss of value, since a restored item cannot be considered to be of equal value with a perfect piece. The difference in value should be added to the cost of restoration in claiming for the compensation due.

Restoration

While obviously it is preferable to buy an item in undamaged, unrestored condition, very occasionally something may be offered which, though not pristine, is so rare that it is unlikely to be available again. In that case a collector may feel that for the sake of acquiring a unique piece, damage is acceptable.

If the damage is minor, say, a hairline crack which will be virtually invisible if the item is carefully placed, restoration may be inappropriate and unnecessary.

If the damage is unsightly, skilled restoration — which is costly — may be considered essential. Naturally, the damage will have been taken into consideration in fixing the price of the piece. Restoration will not bring the item back to the value of a perfect piece, though it will improve the appearance and so make it more desirable.

Restoration on an item reduces its value by around a third, though this is obviously only a very rough guide and the amount of restoration will vary from piece to piece. Also, of course, some restorers are much more skilled than others, the best being frighteningly competent.

For this reason it is important to be able to trust the dealers from whom items are bought. Reputable dealers will always frankly point out any damage and/or restoration and price pieces accordingly.

That said, standards vary enormously and the collector needs to be clear as to what is acceptable to him. Some collectors reject anything that is less than mint condition, while others can happily live with minor chips on the back of a plate which will look fine once hung on the wall.

Wear from use is another matter again, and since Susie Cooper's lithographed work is fairly readily available, it seems sensible to look out for pieces where the central lithographed motif is not faded or worn.

Crazing, (the faint cracking of the surface glaze), varies enormously from piece to piece and it is up to the collector to decide how much is too much. If an item is crazed to such an extent it affects the immediate appearance of the piece, it is probably too much. Very slight crazing is perhaps inevitable, being the result of the passage of time.

Handling a piece is probably the best way to assess it, since more can be revealed by touch than by sight. Check handles, spouts, rims and bases for minor damage, while a careful look into the interior of teapots and coffeepots for staining is advisable. It is often possible to remove light staining by standing a solution of detergent or bicarbonate of soda in the pot overnight. An old toothbrush will help for removing stains or dirt from awkward corners.

Susie Cooper's early handpainted patterns are the ones where restoration is most likely to have been carried out to the paintwork, so it is wise to look closely at these with this in mind. Very slight variations in the colour may be detected, as some colours are particularly hard to match. Owing to new Health and Safety regulations certain combinations of pigment are no longer permitted.

Where restoration has taken place to the body of the item, this may be revealed by variations in the surface glaze.

However, it would be unfortunate if the pleasure of collecting came to be spoilt by suspicion. Most dealers are too concerned for their reputation to do anything underhanded, and should any item prove to be unsatisfactory for any reason, they will be prepared to refund the cost in full.

Lighting and Display

Much will depend on the space available to display the collection as it grows. If they harmonise with existing furniture, china cabinets of the period are appropriate and can be found in a variety of woods or veneers, so that it is usually possible to find a suitable one. They have the double advantage of protecting the collection from damage and of cutting down on dusting, which in itself reduces the risk of accidents.

Some china cabinets come with original strip lighting (which must be re-wired) but it is fairly easy to insert lighting if it is needed. If shelves are being made specially, it makes sense to have these of glass as then lighting from the top may be sufficient to light the whole display.

If the shelves are in a suitable alcove, perhaps one each side of a chimney-breast, sliding glass doors will add protection to the pieces.

For displaying plates, most ironmongers and DIY shops sell plate-hangers in a variety of sizes, but it is important to choose those with plastic-covered hooks to avoid damage to the rim of the plate or to the paint-work.

For wall-plates or plaques, special heavy-duty plate-hangers are available in very large sizes. Though these are expensive compared with the usual hangers, it is a wise precaution to use them.

Generally speaking, pieces from the same period of Susie Cooper's career or in the same idiom look attractive grouped together. Alternatively, colour-blocking to match a colour scheme can be very effective.

Because much of Susie Cooper's work was in advance of her time, it will fit equally well into traditional or modern interiors. Modern display cases with spotlighting will set off most of her work to its best advantage, especially the larger pieces.

While Susie Cooper's seed paintings are sold for large sums of money and so are out of reach of the average collector, posters of exhibitions of her work are more moderately priced, and suitably framed would make an appropriate background to a display of her work.

Recently a range of cushion covers has been made available based on designs by Susie Cooper for tapestry or felt appliqué and these would also enhance a collection made up for use in the room where it is housed.

Table-lamps by Susie Cooper are sometimes found and would naturally be the perfect lighting in a room where a collection of her work is on display.

Rarity

Tableware from any pottery has always been made in much greater quantity than 'fancies' — that is, decorative items intended for display rather than for practical use. However, because of the hazards of everyday use, tableware tends to get broken on a regular basis, while fancies are often preserved by being handled with more care and kept in safer places.

Because Susie Cooper's name has been familiar to the buying public for so long, as synonymous with quality and value, it is less likely that in periods of changing taste her work was disposed of to jumble sales or charity shops, and collectors may find that it has been stored away in the cupboards and attics of elderly relatives who changed to a modern alternative but felt their original Susie Cooper pieces too good to let go.

The publicity surrounding Susie Cooper's recent ninetieth birthday as well as the rise in interest in the Art Deco period generally, fostered by the media and by films and television has made people aware that if they have Susie Cooper pottery or china in their homes, this could now be brought on to the market to satisfy current collecting demands.

While post-war shapes and patterns remain in good supply and pre-war lithographed tableware is fairly easy to find, the early hand-painted items, the incised ware and Susie Cooper's work for Gray's all tend to be much rarer. This is especially true of lustre ware, which is difficult to find in good condition and is expensive when found.

Shape also is a factor, the Kestrel shape being particularly popular, probably because its 'double' spout makes it instantly recognisable.

Among the hand-painted patterns, those featuring animals, especially the leaping deer which has been particularly identified with Susie Cooper since she used it as her trade mark for so many years, and those featuring people, like the golfer, the skier and the clown, are extremely sought after and fetch high prices at auction.

Similarly, geometric patterns either in vivid shades like the black, green, red, blue and yellow **Moon and Mountain** or the more subtle colour combinations of her early Crown Works days, are very popular with collectors and are always expensive as a result.

Sets of items, for example, *Tea for Two* sets or *Breakfast in Bed* sets, tend to be more expensive as a set than they would be if the cost of individual items were added together. This is especially so if it is clear from provenance or from the matching of the backstamp and paintress' mark throughout that the set is not 'made up' but has been together from its manufacture.

With such a very wide range of patterns to choose from, it seems likely that items can be found with comparative ease to complement any colour scheme and it is up to collectors to decide if they feel it would be appropriate to go for quantity or quality. Decorating a kitchen, for instance, in a vast array of, say **Dresden Spray** or **Printemps**, can look extremely effective, while in a sitting room a single piece of incised ware can be sufficient to provide the perfect focal point.

Probably one of the most enjoyable methods of collecting is to side-step the hype of expensive 'collectable' patterns and choose a theme which particularly appeals — the sea, perhaps, or a selection of favourite flowers — and collect items related to that theme, buying as a rule the more reasonably priced items, with an occasional special piece when funds permit.

Availability

Collecting, like any other hobby, demands much more than mere spending-power. Time, thought and effort have gone into every major collection and a well-balanced selection of items will give much greater pleasure than sheer bulk.

Having decided upon the direction the collection is to take, and backed this up by reading all that relates to the subject, the next step is to find out what is available locally. Some dealers now specialise in items from the Twenties and Thirties and among them there may be several who deal primarily in Susie Cooper, just as there are some shops which sell almost exclusively Clarice Cliff. Having identified the dealers with a Susie Cooper bias, it should be possible to arrange to be informed when items particularly needed to fill gaps in the collection become available.

Such dealers, and other collectors one meets with in the course of dealing with them, may then be the source of information about Susie Cooper outlets further afield. These may be shops, stalls in antique markets or fairs. In turn the fairs may be general, with a proportion of Art Deco stalls, or specialist Art Deco fairs of which there are an increasing number taking place regularly through the year.

Events advertised locally such as school fetes or charity bazaars with bric-a-brac stalls are worth visiting on the principle that even today not everybody is aware of the collectability of Susie Cooper items and some of her work may have been put out, perhaps without having been recognised for what it is. It is well worth paying perhaps a little more than asked, always provided of course that the condition warrants it, in order to build up a good relationship with the organisers, so that in future they may watch out for items of interest. The same is true of charity shops, where a regular and generous customer will be regarded as worth cultivating.

Magazines for collectors carry details of fairs, auctions and shops as well as having classified columns for collectors' advertisements. It is best, of course, to be fairly specific about requirements, otherwise items may be offered ranging from early Gray's pieces through to patterns seventy years later for Wedgwood, many unsuitable for the collection in mind.

Probably the most helpful and productive source of information and advertising is the magazine published by the Susie Cooper Collectors' Group. The Group exists to promote the exchange of information and items between collectors and as each collection takes a slightly different angle from every other it is unwise to regard other collectors as rivals, since co-operation can result in many satisfactory deals and exchanges.

As interest and enthusiasm grows, it may be appropriate to consider studying the trade press. The major organ of the trade is the *Antiques Trade Gazette*, which is available on subscription only, and is weekly. Also weekly is the *Antiques Bulletin*, available mainly by subscription but frequently sold at fairs, while *Antiques Today* is monthly, available by subscription but sold in shops, markets and fairs.

Many collectors are wary of auctions but it should be remembered that the private collector can afford to pay slightly more for pieces than the dealers who have to bear in mind overheads and profit-margins. That said, the buyer's premium adds to all successful bids at most auction houses.

Specialist Susie Cooper auctions now take place at Christie's in London and may be regarded as an accurate guide to price trends, except when artificially high prices result from a personality clash where two people get locked into a bidding battle. Apart from this, the occasions can be very instructive and often modest bids secure desirable items. For those unable to attend, a catalogue obtained before hand and then priced up from a list of sale results, obtainable afterwards, provides a very useful price guide to use in future transactions.

Local auction houses usually include a run-down on items coming up in the sales they advertise and provided the pottery has been scrutinised thoroughly when viewing the auction, bargains can sometimes be had on occasions when no local dealers are looking particularly for Susie Cooper pieces.

If other commitments prevent attendance in person at auctions, it is usually possible to secure the services of one of the porters, who will bid according to instructions in return for a small tip when successful.

As well as allowing for the disposal of surplus items, the occasional taking of a stall at an antique fair may prove worthwhile as Susie Cooper pottery being put out for sale elsewhere in the venue can be seen before the public is admitted. It is also probably worth paying the higher 'trade admission' charged now at many of the larger fairs which allows the collector entrance along with trade buyers before the fair is open to the general public. That said, it is worth keeping a sharp eye open for items which emerge later in the day as sales cause gaps on stalls and fresh stock is put out. It is a mistake to assume all the best goes first.

Particularly with Susie Cooper, it is worth letting as many people as possible both in the trade and outside it know that items are being sought, since friends may have other friends or relatives with Susie Cooper pottery available.

Because of this factor, once the collection gets well under way, further publicity can be useful, such as articles in the local press or in collectors' magazines. Caution is advisable, of course, and it is unwise to be too free with information such as exact address or telephone numbers. The journalist concerned will be willing to act as intermediary in case of bone fide offers, which can sometimes be of great interest.

Fakes

So far there has been no major cause for concern regarding fake items of Susie Cooper pottery. Obviously it is not worthwhile to fake items unless they are very valuable, the cost of the exercise outweighing the potential gain, and generally speaking the expensive pieces are sold either by very reputable dealers or by major auction houses, where provenance and authenticity are guaranteed.

While considerable quantities of Susie Cooper pottery continue to be available, it seems unlikely that fakes will be a viable proposition. It is far more likely that damaged items will be restored and passed off as perfect or that worn paint will be replaced, and these are the areas in which collectors should exercise caution.

Since the backstamps used throughout Susie Cooper's career have been extremely well documented, any variation which is unfamiliar should be treated with suspicion until authenticity is proved. As in many other collecting situations, the guiding principle must be, 'If in doubt, don't buy it!'

Reproductions

So far reproductions of Susie Cooper pottery have not been produced, but at the time of the 1987 Victoria and Albert Museum's travelling exhibition, Wedgwood re-issued three Susie Cooper patterns on the Kestrel shape.

These were on show at the time of the exhibition so that orders could be taken, but, attractive as they were, they were not considered to be a commercial success, perhaps because collectors felt that they preferred to put out their money on original pieces rather than on re-issues of earlier shapes and patterns.

Wedgwood have already begun a series of high-quality reproductions of the work of Clarice Cliff so it seems quite probable that eventually it will be considered appropriate to offer a similar range based on the work of Susie Cooper. When and if that day comes, and it seems unlikely to be for some years yet, collectors will have to make the same decision Clarice Cliff collectors have had to make — whether or not to include modern replicas among original work, whether to buy them and keep them as a separate section of the collection, or whether to avoid them altogether.

Auction Trends

For some years, Susie Cooper items have been appearing in sales of twentieth century decorative arts held by the major auction houses in London and elsewhere, but generally these were pieces which fell into the 'art pottery' category, that is, large vases and plaques either from the lustre ware ranges or studio ware, incised or hand-painted, and these naturally fetched high prices, being rare and impressive. Otherwise, items like tableware, whether lithographed or hand-painted, or nursery ware, were generally sold at minor auctions and regarded as run-of-the-mill. Then in 1991 an auction was held at Christie's South Kensington at which the morning was devoted to work by Susie Cooper and the afternoon to Clarice Cliff pottery. Christie's had been holding one-day Clarice Cliff sales for some years, and these were regarded as being the highspot of the year for Clarice Cliff collectors. That Susie Cooper was acknowledged to have a similar devoted following was a major step forward in her increasing popularity. Commercial recognition was being added to scholarly approval. Over one hundred and fifty lots were listed in the catalogue, many illustrated in colour and ranging from a single soup bowl to a Gray's tea-set for six in a geometric pattern. The fact that the estimate for this tea-set was £200-£400 when it fetched over £1500 may indicate that the auction house, while sensing that there was movement in the Susie Cooper market, had not realised quite how much

The following year a similar auction was held but this time less than sixty lots were offered, possibly because increasing enthusiasm for Susie Cooper's work meant that less of the important items were available for auction. However, some superb wall-plates were on offer, fetching between three and five hundred pounds each, while a pair of vases in the *Moon and Mountain* pattern fetched over twelve hundred, including premium.

'Ashmun' cream jug and fancies c2206, circa 1974/75.

'Classic Vista' can jug and covered sugar No. c990, circa 1960.

PRICE AND RARITY GUIDE

With such a long period of production and such a wide range of shapes and patterns, to give guidance as to possible prices for Susie Cooper items is difficult in the extreme, but as always rarity is a major factor. Other basic guidelines are obvious — most collectors prefer hand-painted pieces to those decorated with lithographs, while in general and for the present only, pre-war items are considered more collectable than post-war pieces, which leads to the preference for earthenware rather than bone china. Again, the Kestrel shape is particularly popular, perhaps because it is so easy recognisable with its 'double' spout.

That said, other factors may be operating to affect a transaction, for example if a lithographed item is needed to complete a set, the purchaser may be willing to pay more for it than the casual collector simply adding another minor item to a widely-based collection. From the seller's point of view, a regular customer may warrant a concessionary price as against that asked from a purchaser never met up with before. These and similar instances apart, the essential ingredient in a transaction is that both parties should feel satisfied with it, neither grudging nor aggrieved.

Collecting and dealing usually involves an on-going relationship based on trust, built up over a period of time and a history of fair transactions. It must also be borne in mind that the market is affected by a variety of transitory circumstances — an article in the national press, a repeat showing of the popular Channel Four series 'Pottery Ladies', high prices reported as being achieved at auction, or even jitters on the Stock Exchange. Dealers, too, have their ups and downs from time to time, sometimes feeling a smaller profit in the hand to be better than a potentially larger one later — perhaps much later! — while overheads vary from place to place and inevitably these affect price-levels.

What follows are general guidelines only, and assume good condition throughout. Nothing should be taken to be hard and fast rules, for just as it is very unwise to be dogmatic about pottery production, exceptions popping up the minute anyone says 'They always did this' or 'They never did that', so it would be foolish to dictate a code of prices as immutable as the laws of the Medes and Persians. Price range 1 covers those patterns made in quantity and so easy to find, price range 2 covers patterns produced briefly or made in smaller quantities and price range 3 indicates patterns or shapes which are rare and very collectable. All three price ranges apply in the main to earthenware, since at present post-war items are still to be found at very modest prices, surfacing at house clearances, charity shops and flea-markets, though it is obvious that the lustre ware of the late 1970s, expensive in its own day, is always going to retain and later increase in value, while classic post-war patterns like that produced for the Royal Pavilion at the Festival of Britain in 1951 will command high prices from collectors keen to build up a representative collection spanning the whole of Susie Cooper's distinguished career.

Carved or Incised Ware

The cost of this varies according to the size of the item and its decorative subject, bowls ranging from £80/$160 to £150/$300 and jugs from £80/$160 to £200/$400. Vases usually cost over £100/$200 and may be as much as £250/$500, decoration of squirrels, rams, etc being generally preferred to leaves and flowers, or simple curves or scrolls. In the main, deeper, richer colours are probably more popular.

Matt Glazed Ware

This range owes its appeal to sophisticated muted colours, simple flowing shapes and the soft, pearly sheen of the matt glazes. The price for these items ranges from £75-£125/$150-$250 for jugs, £60-£100/$120-$200 for bowls and £80-£200/$160-$400 for vases, according to size. Like Incised ware, the matt glazed ware has the attraction of studio pottery and is effective when displayed singly or grouped together.

Nursery ware

At present this is very popular and fetches high prices, a *Kestrel* shape Nursery ware cocoa pot and cover fetching nearly £300 at the Christie's specialist Susie Cooper auction on 12th November 1992, while the previous year a similar item but in the very rare **Skier** pattern went for £660. A three-inch Nursery ware mug, 'Dignity and Impudence', with two amusing dogs confronting each other, went for £275 in 1991, a 'Horse and Jockey' plate for £132 and a Nursery ware lamp base for £209. It is obvious why Nursery ware is rare, since it was subject to even more hazards in use than everyday tableware. It also has a nostalgic appeal recalling childhood days and favourite pieces of nursery pottery. While purists may feel it lacks the sophistication of Susie Cooper's designs for adults, it nevertheless has a sturdy charm and is well-designed in attractive colours, portraying realistic animals in humorous and endearing ways, eschewing the anthropomorphism of furry creatures clad in human dress.

TABLE WARE AND RELATED ITEMS

Group 1: Lithographed patterns, simple banded patterns, hand-painted items with minimal decoration.
Group 2: Hand-painted, tube-lined and sgraffito decoration.
Group 3: Lustre ware, cubist and geometric hand-painted, pictorial hand-painted in short order patterns.

	Group 1
Teapot Large	£55-£75/$150-$210
Teapot Small	£45-£65/$130-$190
Milk jug + Sugar basin	£35-£65/$104-$190
Trio (cup, saucer teaplate)	£25-£45/$70-$130
Teacup & saucer	£15-£25/$44-$70
Coffee cup & saucer	£20-£30/$60-$90
Coffee pot	£55-£75/$150-$210
Plate 5"	£7-£12/$20-$36
Plate 7"	£8-£13/$24-$38
Plate 8"	£10-£15/$30-$50
Plate 9"	£13-£18/$38-$54
Plate 10"	£15-£20/$44-$80
Large fruit dish	£30-£40/$90-$120
Fruit dish 5"	£15-£20/$44-$60
Tureen, cover	£45-£55/$130-$160
Sauce tureen, cover, ladle saucer	£65-£85/$190-$240

Group 2

£100-£200/$300-£600

£75-£150/$210-$450

£55-£95/$150-$280

£50-£100/$150-$200

£30-£65/$90-$190

£35-£55/$94-$150

£100-£200/$300-$600

£15-£30/$40-$90

£18-£35/$54-$90

£20-£40/$60-$90

£25-£50/$70-$150

£30-£60/$90-$180

£60-£90/$180-$270

£25-£50/$70-$150

£65-£85/$190-$240

£75-£95/$210-$290

Group 3

£250-£450/$650-$1350

£150-£300/$450-$900

£150/£250/$450-$650

£150-£300/$450-$900

£95-£150/$280-$450

£65-£95/$190-$280

£250-£450/$650-$1350

£55-£75/$150-$210

£75-£100/$210-$300

£85-£100/$250-$300

£95-£120/$280-$360

£125-£150/$324-$450

£100-£150/$300-$450

£65-£90/$190-$270

£100-£150/$300-$450

£100-£150/$300-$450

Group 1: Lithographed patterns, simple banded patterns, hand-painted items with minimal decoration.
Group 2: Hand-painted, tube-lined and sgraffito decoration.
Group 3: Lustre ware, cubist and geometric hand-painted, pictorial hand-painted in short order patterns.

	Group 1
Meat dishes, edge decoration only	
Large	£35-£50/$94-$150
Medium	£30-£40/$90-$120
Small	£25-£35/$74-$104
Gravy boat with saucer	£25-£35/$74-$104
Soup or pudding dish	£18-£25/$54-$74
Covered soup bowl with saucer	£15-£25/$44-$74
Chargers, wall plaques, decorative wall plates	£65-£120/$190-$290
Larger jugs (Paris shape etc)	£25-£35/$74-$104
Biscuit barrels	£65-£85/$190-$254
Lamp base	£65-£150/$210-$290
Vase	—
Novelty items such as cheese dish, muffin dish, egg cup set, ash tray,	£35-£100/$104-$160
Candle holders, cocktail trays etc.	£70-£120/$210-$360

Group 2

£45-£60/$130-$180
£40-£55/$120-$160
£35-£50/$74-$150
£40-£65/$120-$190
£25-£35/$74-$104
£25-£35/$74-$104

£75-£150/$210-$450

£35-£75/$104-$210
£95-£125/$290-$324
£100-£150/$300-$450
£75-£150/$210-$450
£75-£125/$210-$374

Group 3

£100-£150/$300-$450
£90-£120/$270-$360
£80-£100/$240-$300
£85-£100/$250-$300
£55-£95/$154-$290
£55-£95/$154-$290

£200-£750/$600-$2200

£125-£350/$324-$1040
£150-£450/$450-$1340
£200-£650/$600-$2000
£200-£650/$600-$2000
£150-£350/$450-$1040

PATTERN DATES — A GENERAL GUIDE

With an output stretching over seven decades, and a total of over four and a half thousand patterns, it is clearly impossible here to list every pattern ever made in all its variations. The following is a general guide, indicating the date of initial production of as many named patterns as possible. Those given later names by collectors are indicated by bold italic type.

1923
Gloria Lustre items, florals and fruit
Fruit Border
Dragon

1924
Gloria Lustre items, birds and
    animals, cherubs

1925
Gloria Lustre items, florals and fruit

1926
Gloria Lustre items, florals and fruit

1927
Vine
Oranges
Bird on a Twig
Other fruit and floral motifs

1928
Acorns
Golden Catkin
Almond Blossom
Quadrupeds

Primula
This is the House that Jack Built
Iris
Lupins
Floral and banded items
Moon and Mountains

1929
Cubist
Silver Palm
Daffodils
Crocus patterns
Layebands
Harmony
Pastoral
Hawaiian
Thistle
Blue Lupins
Persian Bird
Birds
Summertime
Floral, geometric and abstract
    patterns

1930
Bronze Chrysanthemums and

other floral patterns including Tulips, Bluebell and Marigolds
Golden Corn
Yellow Fruit
Persian
Spots
Banded, abstract and geometric items

1931

More floral patterns — Rose, Daisy, Marsh Marigold etc
Symphony
The Storm
The Pasture
Rooster
Deer Leap
Banded abstract and geometric items
Scarlet Runner Beans
Tadpoles
Hunting Subjects
Rabbit
Galaxy
Feather

1932

A very prolific year — floral motifs like Chintz Spray, Nosegay, Shepherd's Purse, Briar Rose
Figural patterns like Balloon Man/Flower Seller, Spanish Dancer/Mexican, Clown
Animal and bird patterns — Tigers, Monkey, Woodpecker, Red Fox

Caravan
Rodeo
Wreath of Flowers
A Country Bunch
Landscape, incised, floral, abstract, geometric and banded items including Wedding Ring

1933

Graduated Black Bands
Yellow Flower
Florida
Killlarney
Little Bo-Beep
Abstract motifs, scrolls, swirls and circles, playing card motifs and floral patterns like Gilley Flower, Pink Hydrangea, landscapes and tube-lined patterns

1934

Pink Carnation
Harebell
Silver Fern
Polka Dot
Scroll
Crayon Line
Egyptian motifs, dots, circles, banded, tube-lined and crayon patterns

1935

Circle and Dash
Two Leaf Spray
Leaves

Cromer
Lithographs like Dresden Spray,
  Swansea Spray
Animal motifs, abstract and
  crayon patterns

1936
Wide Buttercups
Blue Primula
Faenza
Horse and Jockey
Noah's Ark
Skier
Floral patterns like Printemps,
  Grey Leaf etc
Animal patterns like Black Pom
  and Tango Terrier, Dignity and
  Impudence etc
Banded, crayon and
  aerographed patterns
Abstract motifs like Exclamation
  Mark, Crescent, etc

1937
Colour variations on established
  patterns
Aerographed, sgraffito
  decoration, banded patterns
Sepia
Ribbon
Nursery ware patterns
Bud motifs & other stylised borders

1938
Endon
Aubergine

Regency Feather
Starbursts
Woodlands
Pineapple
Floral motifs like Patricia Rose,
  Elderberry
Aerographed items

1939
Double' motifs — Leaf and Vine,
  Pears and Apples, Pears and
  Cherries, Pears and Plums,
  Scallop and Curl
Long Leaf
Sage Band
Dog & fowl motifs, feathers & ferns
Beechwood
Aerographed, spotted and
  freehand designs

1940
Fruit and floral motifs,
  aerographed patterns

1941
Tulip and Daisy Spray
Pink Aster Spray
Tigerlily
Vine Leaf
Cornflower

1942
Starburst
Bud
Seaweed
Sgraffito and aerographed items

1946
Tree of Life
Bud and Ring
Starburst 2
Aerographed patterns

1947
Chinese Fern
Wintersleaf
Michaelmas
Aerographed abstract motifs

1948
Winter Sunshine
Stars
Ladybird
Aerographed patterns

1949
Stars
Spots
Tulip in Pompadour
Pear in Pompadour
Sabrina and Pompadour
Blue Campanula
Aerographed & banded patterns

1950
English Summer
Canabola
White Dahlia

1951
Waterlily
Black Oak Leaf
Peach

China ware introduced
Regency Stripe
Sea Anemone
Astral
Australian Wild Flower Series
Nutmeg Tree
Persian Rose
Stars, floral and bird motifs

1952
Forget-me-not Blue
Azalea
Gardenia
Magnolia
Clematis
Wreath Border
Bracken
Fruit motifs
China ware
Floral motifs, colour variations on
   established patterns

1953
Everlasting Life
Blue Orchid
Colour variations on established
   patterns
China ware
Aerographed decorations
Star motifs

1954
No earthenware
China ware
Whispering Grass
One o'clock

Colour variations on several
  established patterns

1955
Richmond Rose
Graduated Lines
China ware
Parrot Tulip
Scroll
Circles
Ring and Dot
Bud

1956
Highland Grass
Blue Fern
Sienna Pastel
Olive Pastel
Black Spot
Stars
Leaf
Petronella
Rubber-stamped motifs
China ware
Charcoal Skeleton Leaf and
  other aerographed patterns
Serpentine Banding and other
  aerographed and sgraffito
  patterns

1957
Brown Feather
Green Feather
Black Feather
Bird
Charcoal Skeleton Leaf

China ware
Corinthian
Romanesque
Palladian
Sheraton
Pomme D'or

1958
Spirals
Meadow Sweet
Carefree
China ware
Confetti
Relief Polka Dot
Shaded Harlequin
Teazle
Black Fruit
Blue Ivy
Romance

1959
Ferndown
Hazelwood
Acanthus
Simplicity
Windfall
Pink Campion
Cornfly
Camelia
Candy Stripe
Gooseberry
New Nut
Elderberry
Parrot Tulip
Blue Gentian

China ware
Hyde Park and other covercoat
  patterns
Colour variations on established
  patterns
Lady Smock and other new
  transfer patterns

1960
Established floral patterns
China ware
Wild Rose
Classic Vista
Margaret Rose, Glen Mist and
  other covercoat patterns
Colour variations on established
  patterns

1961
Established floral and fruit patterns
Daffodils
Amaryllis
Colour variations of established
  patterns
China ware
Universal Fruit and other covercoat
  motifs, some for export to USA

1962
No earthernware produced
Blue Rose, Blue Peony and other
  covercoat floral motifs plus
  colour variations of established
  patterns

1964
Floriana
Rhythm
Modesty
Squares
Ovals
Lady Barbara
Penelope
Serenity
There were no earthenware
  patterns after July 1964
China ware
Lady Barbara
Penelope
White Wedding
Apple Gay and other covercoat
  motifs
Colour variations on established
  patterns

1965
Broken Stripes
Vintage
Nasturtium
Venetia
Moselle and other covercoat
  motifs, plus colour variations

1966
Garland
Art Nouveau
Autumn Leaves and Berry
Athena
Jason
Distinctive
Iris

Carnation
Colour Variations
(Wedgwood)

1967
Covercoat patterns including
    Mercury, Neptune, Andromeda,
    Saturn and Heraldry
Greensleeves for W. Adams & Sons

1968
Carnaby Daisy
Harlequinade
Autumn Leaves
Keystone
Nebula and other covercoat
    patterns, plus colour variations

1969
Diablo
Pennant
Colour variations

1970
Colosseum
Florida
Cressida
Spartan

1971
Columbine
Cornpoppy
Camelia
Charisma
Indian Summer
Everglade

Lucerne
Black Eyed Susan
Banded patterns and covercoat
    motifs

1976
Chou Dynasty
Floral Bouquet (Silver Jubilee
    pattern) with silver lustre
    decoration – the wheel coming
    full circle from her Gloria Lustre
    for Grays

1977
Variation on Floral Bouquet
English Wildflower series

1979
Birds of the World
Iris and other floral patterns

1982
Blue Daisy

1983
Meadowlands
Inspiration
Stardust

1984
Blue Haze
Florida

Goblets 'Gold Star' mid to late 1950s.

Collection of mid-1950s items.

'Black Fruit' TV set No. c897, circa 1958.

'Nebula' No. c2135/8, circa 1969

'Keystone' can teapots No. c2131/2.

'Assyrian motif' Quail jug No. c1010.

A SUSIE COOPER CHRONOLOGY

1902 29th October — Susie Cooper born at Stansfield near Burslem, the youngest of seven children of John and Mary-Ann Cooper.

1914 February — John Cooper died and his family moved to Milton.

1917 After leaving school, Susie Cooper helped in the family business.

1918 September — Enrolled at Burslem School of Art for evening classes in freehand drawing, plant drawing and cookery.

1919 Awarded a scholarship for full-time training at the school. Gordon Forsyth, formerly art director at Minton Hollins and the Pilkington Tile & Pottery Company, Principal of the City Schools of Art, encouraged her. He became Superintendant of Art Education the following year.

1922 June (sometimes given as 1923) — Joined Gray's Pottery in order to qualify for a scholarship to the Royal College of Art in London. Decided instead to stay on in the pottery industry.

1923 Working on piece-work, Susie Cooper painted the lions on the Gloria Lustre range exhibited on the Gray's stand at the B.I.F. Promoted to resident designer. Backstamp incorporating her name introduced (used until 1931) September/October: Exhibition, Victoria & Albert Museum, 'British Industrial Art, Recent Examples of British Pottery', included pattern 2866, her own floral design.

1924 Items designed by Susie Cooper shown at the British Empire Exhibition, Wembley.

1925 Exposition des Arts Décoratifs et Industriels Modernes, Paris, items designed by Susie Cooper shown on Gray's stand in the British Pavilion.

1928 'Golden Catkin', 'Almond Blossom', 'Quadrupeds', 'This is the House that Jack Built', using the print and enamel technique. Banded ware and geometric designs, including Cubist Designed shape of coffee pot, teapot, milk jug and sugar basin, Johnson Brothers Ltd, making the coffee pot for Gray's and Lancaster and Sons the other items.

1929 Layebands, created for the West End actress Evelyn Laye and sold by Heal's. 'Thistle', also for Heal's was designed but not on sale until the following year.
Design of screen curtains for the Odeon Cinema, Marble Arch, commissioned by Skilhorn and Edwards, a leading London interior design company.
29th October — Susie Cooper left Gray's Pottery.
Premises rented at the George Street Pottery, Tunstall, but closed after three weeks by the bankruptcy of the landlord.

1930 Chelsea Works, Moorland Road, Burslem, rented from Doulton & Co.
April — first advertisement in *Pottery Gazette & Glass Trades Review*. Floral patterns like 'Bronze Chrysanthemums', 'Tulips', 'Carnations' and 'Marigolds', as well as small stylised patterns like 'Peacock Feathers'. 'Symphony', 'Spots', 'Exclamation mark' and also banded patterns. Black triangle mark in use (until 1932)

1931 B.I.F. stand very successful and at invitation of Harry Wood moved in August to second floor of the Crown Works, Newcastle Street, Burslem. Lively patterns like 'Runner Beans', 'Tadpoles' and 'Galaxy' followed.

1932 Leaping Deer backstamp introduced (used till mid-1960s).
'Nosegay', 'Freesia', 'Woodpecker' and various characters and animals used as motifs. The 'Kestrel' shape launched at the B.I.F. 'Wedding Ring' ordered by John Lewis, the department store.
The London showroom was opened in October. Incised studio ware proved popular.
Susie Cooper was elected to the North Staffordshire branch of the Council of the Society of Industrial Artists.

1933 April — Susie Cooper became a director of Bursley Ltd.
The Kestrel tureen, with reversible lid, was introduced, as well as the 'Curlew' shape. Invited to exhibit at the Dorland Hall Exhibition of Industrial Art in Relation to the Home. Stylised floral patterns and abstract motifs featured.

1934 Tube-lining was used as decoration. A range of wall-masks was made. 'Polka Dots' and 'Crayon' patterns were popular.

1935 Exhibited at the Royal Academy's 'British Art in Industry' exhibition.
'Wren' and 'Jay' shapes designed for Woods and 'Rex' and 'Classic' shapes modified. Lithography introduced — 'Dresden Spray', 'Nosegay' and 'Swansea Spray'.

1936 New crayon patterns included 'Crayon Loop' and 'Crayon Scallop'. Floral patterns included 'Blue Primula', 'Wide Buttercup', 'Grey Leaf', 'Printemps' and 'Faenza'. Nursery ware featured animals. Other motifs included 'Horse and Jockey', 'Golfer' and 'Skier'.

1937 Bursley Ltd was renamed the Susie Cooper Pottery Ltd
'Falcon' shape launched.

1938 'Spiral' shape launched. Patterns included 'Endon' and 'Patricia Rose' and also aerographing with sgraffito.

1939 Fruit patterns were very successful.
Susie Cooper was made a Royal Designer for Industry.

1940 Despite wartime restrictions, new patterns were launched including 'Black Leaves', 'Tulip', 'Daisy Spray', 'Pink Aster Spray' and 'Tigerlily'.

1942 'Bud' and 'Seaweed' were among the patterns launched, but a serious fire then ended production until after the war.

1946 When rebuilding allowed resumption of production, shortage of lithographs, stocks of which had been destroyed by the fire, led to hand-painted, aerographed and sgraffito patterns using motifs based on leaves and berries, seaweed and flowers. 'Tree of Life' was a particularly successful pattern.
Susie Cooper was invited to join the selection committee for the 'Britain Can Make It' exhibition.

1948 'Tulip in Pompadour' and 'Pear in Pompadour' were typical of the new contemporary style of patterns now produced.

1950 In order to expand china production, Susie Cooper bought the Jason China Company of Longton.
The 'Quail' shape was designed for the Festival of Britain. Lithography was revived for floral patterns like 'Gardenia', 'Magnolia' and 'Orchid'.

1951 Quail coffee sets were commissioned for the Royal Pavilion at the Festival of Britain. Patterns now included 'Astral', 'Gold Bud', 'Sea Anemone' and 'Faenza'

1956 The Fluted shape, a version of Quail, was launched. Strong classical patterns included 'Palladian', 'Corinthian', 'Romanesque', 'Pomme D'or' and 'Highland Grass'.

1957 The Scallop shape was launched at the Blackpool Fair, but shortly afterwards a second fire caused considerable damage.

1958 Despite this, Susie Cooper designed the Can shape, destined to be an all-time favourite over the next three decades. A merger with R. H. and S. L. Plant was negotiated, to facilitate the planned switch to bone china and the phasing out of earthenware. Popular patterns included 'Hyde Park' and 'Black Fruit'.

1959 Susie Cooper bought the Crown Works. 'Spirals', 'Meadowsweet' and 'Carefree' were launched.

1964 By now the change over to china was complete. Typical patterns of the early 1960s were 'Glen Mist', 'Venetia', 'Talisman' and 'Apple Gay'.

1966 Josiah Wedgwood and Sons now took over both companies, Susie Cooper continuing as designer for her own company, producing designs like 'Cornflower', 'Champagne', 'Pimpernel' and 'Mariposa'.

1967 This year was notable for many vivid covercoat patterns like the popular 'Carnaby Daisy', 'Harlequinade', 'Autumn Leaves' and 'Keystone'.

1971 'Cornpoppy', perhaps the most familiar of all the post-war patterns, was launched at the Blackpool Fair.

1972 Susie Cooper resigned as director of Susie Cooper Limited.

1976 The wheel came full circle as Susie Cooper designed lustre ware to celebrate the Silver Jubilee of the Queen the following year.

1978 A retrospective exhibition of Susie Cooper's work was held by Wedgwood at the Sanderson's Exhibition Gallery in London, entitled 'Elegance and Utility'.

1979 Susie Cooper was awarded the Order of the British Empire in recognition of her services to the British pottery industry.

1980 Closure of the Crown Works by Wedgwood. Susie Cooper moved her studio to William Adams in Tunstall.

1982 Stoke-on-Trent City Museum and Art Gallery mounted an exhibition of her work to celebrate Susie Cooper's 80th birthday.

1985 A Channel 4 television series 'Pottery Ladies' saluted the work of Clarice Cliff, Charlotte Rhead and Susie Cooper. Extremely popular, it has been repeated several times since.

1987 Under the title 'Susie Cooper Productions', the Victoria and Albert Museum launched a travelling exhibition of her work, in association with which Wedgwood revived three 1930s patterns on breakfast sets in the Kestrel shape.
Susie Cooper was awarded an Honourary Doctorate, its highest honour, by the Royal College of Art.

1990 An exhibition of Susie Cooper's seed paintings was held at Stoke-on-Trent City Museum and Art Gallery, travelling later to a London Gallery.

1992 Susie Cooper's ninetieth birthday was celebrated by Wedgwood by an exhibition of her work at their Visitors Centre, Barlaston. Susie Cooper herself celebrated by producing a limited edition of ninety of a porcelain model of a leaping deer.

ANTIQUE MARKETS, SPECIALIST SHOPS AND FAIRS

Alfie's Antique Market 13/25 Church Street, London NW8
Nick Jones and Geoffrey Peake, G0 70-4, Beth G0 43/44)
Antiquarius 235 Kings Road, London SW**3**
Art Deco Ceramics Howard and Pat Watson
Stalls 3 & 4, Stratford Antique Centre,
Ely Street, Stratford-upon-Avon
CV37 6LN
Beverley 30 Church Street, London NW8 8EP
Bizarre Decorative Arts 116 Manchester Road, Altrincham,
Cheshire WA14 4PY
Chenil Galleries 181 Kings Road, London SW3
Alexandra Palace Fair, Wood Green, London N22
700 stalls, many selling Susie Cooper
ceramics

Kensington Decorative Arts Fair Kensington Town Hall, London W8

National Art Deco Fair Loughborough Town Hall,
Loughborough
Leicestershire

Sandown Park Esher, Surrey
Afternoon and evening fair

South of England Art Deco Fair Brighton Centre, Brighton W. Sussex
Wakefield Fairs

Warwick Art Deco Fair Hilton Hotel, Warwick

Susie Cooper Collectors Group PO Box 48, Beeston
Nottingham NG9 2RN

BIBLIOGRAPHY

Elegance and Utility Adrian Woodhouse, Wedgwood, 1978
Susie Cooper Productions Ann Eatwell, Publications Department, Victoria and Albert Museum, London, 1987
Susie Cooper Ceramics, A Collectors Guide Andrew Casey, Jazz Publications, 1992
Susie Cooper Adrian Woodhouse, Trilby Books, 1992
Handpainted Grays Pottery Paul Niblett, City Museum and Art Gallery, Stoke-on-Trent, 1982
Art Deco Tableware Judy Spours, Ward Lock, 1988
A Collector's History of English Pottery Griselda Lewis, Antique Collectors Club, 1985
Ceramics Frances Hannah, Bell & Hyman, Twentieth Century Design series, 1986
Potters and Paintresses Cheryl Buckley, Womens Press, 1990
A Woman's Touch Isabelle Anscombe, 1984

Articles
Susie Cooper, Pride of the Potteries Graham Crossingham-Gower, *Art and Antiques*, 1975
Susie Cooper, OBE, Designer, March 1979
Art Deco Ceramics: England Garth Clark, *Ceramics Monthly*, September 1979
Susie Cooper, Diverse Designer Su Snodin, *Antique Collector*, August 1982
Sixty Glorious Years Neil Fletcher, *Antique Collecting*, October 1984
Our Susie Adrian Woodhouse, *Homes and Gardens*, June 1987
Saluting Susie Cooper Pat Watson, *Antique & Collectors Fayre*, June 1987
Designed for Elegance and Utility Stephen Dale, *Antique Dealer & Collectors Guide*, October 1990
The Story of Susie Cooper, A Living Legend Pat Watson, Antique Bulletin, October 1992

also
Christie's South Kensington, Catalogues, Clarice Cliff and Susie Cooper sales, 7 November 1991, and 12 November 1992.
The Pottery Gazette and Glass Trade Review

A R T · D E C O · C E R A M I C S

UNITS 3/4 STRATFORD ANTIQUE CENTRE ELY STREET STRATFORD-UPON-AVON CV37 6LN 0789 204351/ 299524

BEVERLEY

ART NOUVEAU

ART DECO

Visit our large shop in Central London for an extensive range of 1920s and 1930s ceramics and glass including Carlton Ware, Clarice Cliff, Shelley, Susie Cooper and Keith Murray etc.

Monday-Thursday 11.00-7.00 Friday and Saturday 9.30-7.00
Sundays by appointment

30 Church Street • Marylebone • London NW8
Telephone: 0171-262 1576

Francis Joseph
P U B L I C A T I O N S
'The Collectors Choice'

Detailed price and information guides to British 20th century ceramics with galleries of extensive colour photographs in each. All the collector needs for identifying the wide range of ceramics produced in Britain over the past 100 years.

Collecting British Toby Jugs

History and prices of Toby Jugs from 1770 to the present day. 200 pages full of photographs. **£14.95**

Collecting Carlton Ware

History, price, shape and rarity guide to one of Art Deco's fastest growing collectables. Full of colour. **£16.95**

Collecting Moorcroft

A comprehensive guide to Moorcroft Pottery. Packed with colour, including price, shape and rarity guide. **£16.95**

Collecting Susie Cooper

Comprehensive guide to the work of Susie Cooper, including price, shape and rarity guide. **£16.95**

Collecting Clarice Cliff

History, price, shape and rarity guide to the most collected and most popular of all Deco ceramics. **£16.95**

Collecting Art Deco Ceramics

A collectable book in its own right. History and detailed colour picture gallery of all the major potters of the 1920s and 1930s. **£14.95**

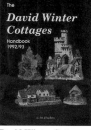

David Winter Cottages Handbook

Price and picture guide to complete output of David Winter Cottages. Do you have one at home? **£14.95**

The Doulton Figure Collectors Handbook

Third edition of this hugely popular book. Price guide and complete listing of valuable Royal Doulton figures. **£12.95**

The Character Jug Collectors Handbook

Sixth edition of our best selling title. Complete listing of Royal Doulton and other 20th Century character jug potters. **£11.95**

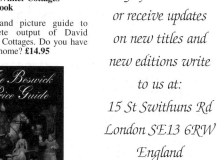

The Beswick Price Guide

Price guide and complete listing of all that is collectable from the Beswick Pottery. **£11.95**

*Prices correct at time of going to press. Please telephone for our latest catalogue.

Notes